www.mascotbooks.com

Let's Pretend This is Normal

©2018 Miriam Verheyden. All Rights Reserved. No part of this publication may be reproduced, stored in a retrieval system or transmitted in any form by any means electronic, mechanical, or photocopying, recording or otherwise without the permission of the author.

I have tried to recreate events, locales, and conversations from my memories of them. I may have changed some identifying characteristics and details, such as physical properties, occupations, and places of residence, and names in order to maintain subject anonymity. My memories are my own, and I have recalled the stories recorded here to the best of my ability.

For more information, please contact:
Mascot Books
620 Herndon Parkway, Suite 320
Herndon, VA 20170
info@mascotbooks.com

Library of Congress Control Number: 2018900739

CPSIA Code: PBANG0118
ISBN-13: 978-1-68401-645-7

Printed in the United States

LET`S PRETEND THIS IS NORMAL

An unlikely love story

Miriam Verheyden

At first, I wanted to dedicate this book to my husband Richard.
But then I remembered that I wrote an entire book about him, so that's enough.
Don't be greedy now.
And anyway, I wrote this for every girl who's ever been lost, scared, heartbroken, and clueless.
I see you; I was you.
Trust me: You will figure it out.

CONTENTS

This book has been inside of me for years. I tried to ignore it. Writing it would be difficult, uncomfortable, and so far out of my comfort zone that my comfort zone would be nothing but a tiny speck in the distance. Yet, it wouldn't leave me alone. It begged to come out. It gnawed at me, filling my waking thoughts and my dreams at night, scratching at my insides.

I was scared. Scared of not being able to do it. Scared of if I did do it, that it would suck. Scared of criticism.

But then I came across two quotes. The first one is from Anne Lamott:

Oh my God, what if you wake up some day, and you're 65, or 75, and you never got your memoir or novel written; or you didn't go swimming in warm pools and oceans all those years because your thighs were jiggly and you had a nice big comfortable tummy; or you were just so strung out on perfectionism and people-pleasing that you forgot to have a big juicy creative life, of imagination and radical silliness and staring off into space like when you were a kid? It's going to break your heart. Don't let this happen.

These words grabbed me, and wouldn't leave me alone. "What if you never got your memoir written..." – I knew, without a doubt, that this would be my big regret in life. From the moment I read those precious words, I knew that I would have to give it a try.

But I was still scared. How to overcome the fear of failure, of being discovered a fraud, of being scrutinized and found lacking?

That's when I found the second quote. It's from my favourite book, Big Magic *by Elizabeth Gilbert. In it, she talks a lot about fear. Turns out, my fear isn't unique; on the contrary, it's the most ordinary and boring fact of life. Everybody is scared. The challenge is finding the courage to go ahead and do the things you are afraid to do, despite the fear.*

That second quote is short, but so powerful that it is the reason you are holding this book in your hands. It goes like this: I'm talking about living a life that is driven more strongly by curiosity than by fear.

That's what I want. A life driven more strongly by curiosity than by fear.

So, on the eve of my 37ᵗʰ birthday, I sat down and began to write the story that wanted to be told:

Our love story.

And, maybe even more importantly, the story of an insecure, lost girl who grew into a confident woman who learnt to love herself. Everything is possible if you let love – and life – transform you.

AUTHOR'S NOTE

Everything in this book is true, at least as true as I remember it. But I have learnt that everybody experiences their own truth. What's true to me will be different for the next person. We are all influenced by our feelings, thoughts, and unique perspectives. Also, I have a terrible memory, so there is a good chance that I unwittingly reshaped history a bit.

I changed some details and the names of people to protect their privacy.

However, my husband's name really is Richard; I had to keep him real. He fell in love with me when I was at my worst, and brought out the best in me.

Without him, this book wouldn't exist.

INTRODUCTION

For most of my life, all I ever wanted was to be normal. Oh, and happy, of course; happy was the next big item on my wish list.

But being normal was the most important one, the big prize. The reason why it was so important to me? Because it always seemed just out of reach.

Growing up, I wasn't one of the weird kids, being neither nerdy, fat, nor obviously different from everybody else. I was never teased or bullied. But as I was growing from a shy child into an awkward but occasionally surprisingly outgoing teenager, one fact became achingly obvious to me: I didn't fit in.

At fifteen, I got my first real kiss and real boyfriend. Finally! It happened in the same night (with the same boy, who do you think I am?), and for two-and-a-half years, we were dating steadily and seriously. At first, I was deliriously happy. I had validation! Having a serious boyfriend meant that you were desirable, never alone, and, of course, *normal.* We were in love, so we talked marriage, kids, a future together. But the longer I stayed with him and learnt about his modest ambitions, the greater my doubts grew. I felt suffocated. His entire family lived in the tiny town I lived in, and contrary to me, he thought that was perfectly fine. In fact, he planned on staying there his entire life!

I couldn't do that. I was desperate to get out! The inevitable happened: we broke up.

Not long after, serious boyfriend #2 came along: a skater boy from my class, seemingly more rebellious, and *much* cooler than my ex. He played in a band! He dyed his goatee pink! He *had* a goatee! We fell in love, got together, and for two-and-a-half years, we were dating steadily and seriously. In fact, this one was more serious than my first relationship; not only did I love him, but we were also best friends. We rarely fought, had tons in common, and he was easy-going, sweet, and supportive. I really wanted it to work out with him. Not only was he great, but I was also friends with his best buds. We hung out together all the time, and I could easily see our future: going from school to college to job, to—where?

Nowhere, I realized to my horror. Incredibly, I had found yet another guy who was perfectly content to stay right where he was, planning on moving into the house next to his parents' where his grandmother currently lived, hopefully with me, so we could go for Sunday dinner to his parents' house every week for the rest of our lives.

No! This couldn't be happening!

Why were these guys so damn happy to stay where they were? Why did none of them want to spread their wings and fly away? Was I the only one? What was wrong with me? Why couldn't I be like everybody else?

Looking around, I found that I was different from the people around me: they seemed happy with their place in life. They didn't show any signs of experiencing the same burning desire to get away like I did; they were content.

I wasn't. I was restless, and unhappy, and clueless about what I wanted in life. I was also alone. While many of my friends didn't know what they wanted to do career-wise, at least they were happy with their surroundings and/or social life. I had none of the above, so with a heavy heart, I broke up with my sweet, gentle, loving boyfriend, feeling like an asshole.

It was horrible. Not only did I lose my best friend, I also lost his posse, which had been *my* posse for the last two-and-a-half years. Now I was truly alone. And for *what*? For a stupid desire to break free? To get out? To experience the world? It wasn't like I was doing that anyway, was I? I was way too timid to do anything about my secret desire to explore the world. Instead, I was moping about, locking myself in my room with my books and my dreams, eating my feelings.

When my parents introduced me to a man they adored, I jumped at the chance. Finding my way on my own obviously hadn't worked; I was lonely, confused, clueless about my future, overweight, and unhappy. Why not try my parents' way? Maybe they really did know better than me!

Turns out, they didn't. Not only did it not work out with the guy, but he hooked up with my sister.

What to do? Staying in my life felt increasingly unbearable, until, one day, I finally couldn't stand it anymore, and I did the scariest thing I could imagine: going on an adventure.

It was one step. One ticket. That first step led me to a small place in the middle of nowhere, 10,000 kilometers away from the place where my life didn't fit.

And there, in the unlikeliest of places, I found the unlikeliest of love stories. Fifteen years later, it is going stronger than ever.

Not only did I find the love of my life, I also found *my* life.

Along the way, I learnt two lessons: create your own normal, and *never* settle.

PROLOGUE

January 10, 2005

I can feel their eyes boring into our backs. Most of them haven't seen him before, and they're understandably curious. They're trying to get a better look at his face, to guess his age.

"Gosh, with that grey beard, he must be at least - in his forties? Or even older? How old is she again …?"

Fortunately for them, the officiant is just getting to that.

"We are gathered together here in the presence of these witnesses to join this man, Richard, born July 12, 1954, and this woman, Miriam, born October 10, 1979, in matrimony, which is an honorable estate, and is not to be entered into unadvisedly or lightly …"

We have lost our audience. Instead of listening, they're busy calculating the difference between our ages, and within seconds, they all get it: twenty-five years. Yup, a quarter of a century.

We can feel the collective intake of breath. The shock. The indignation. Why is she doing this? How dare he?

The service doesn't last long. After we have signed on the dotted line, congratulations are in order.

I wouldn't exactly call them heartfelt. The smiles are too wide, the hugs stiff, the words forced. Everybody seems uncomfortable.

As it turns out, this will be the theme of our wedding: awkward as hell.

For one, it's Monday morning at 11:30. Who gets married on a Monday morning? People who aren't serious about marriage, that's who. At least that seems to be the unspoken agreement of our wedding guests. I can practically see them taking bets under the table about how long this will last; I suspect nobody is giving us to our first anniversary.

But no matter, the farce has begun, it must be completed. Let's just get to the end of today, shall we?

Our wedding party of sixteen is headed to a nearby castle. Calm yourselves, people; it sounds grander than it is. Germany is lousy with castles, and this one isn't the grandiose Disney-version with turrets and high towers and a castle moat; it looks like a large house. But it's pink! Besides, the owners are customers of my parents' produce business, so at least this charade of a wedding makes good business sense.

Before we head inside for lunch, it's time for pictures. We don't have a professional photographer, but my uncle offered this morning to snap a few photos, an offer I'm grateful for. Without him, there would be no record of my wedding day—and the thought occurs to me that this was maybe intended by the wedding planner, my mom? But no matter, Uncle Randy is here to the rescue.

He directs us to line up in front of the pink castle. The pink goes well with my outfit, because if you think I'm wearing a white wedding dress, think again. I'm dressed in a $79 mail-order suit: a skirt-and-jacket number in pink and purple boucle, 'Chanel-inspired,' as my mother described it to me. The skirt is so short it barely covers my ample bottom, and I spend much of the day pulling on my skirt in a desperate (and useless) attempt to make the skirt appear longer.

Why would I have chosen a skirt that makes me so uncomfortable, you may wonder? I'm glad you asked; I didn't.

I may be the only bride in the free world who not only didn't choose her wedding dress, but didn't even see it—or try it on—until the night before the wedding. Talk about living dangerously! Being out of the country at the time of wedding planning, my mother offered to take over the job. Ridiculously thankful to her for seemingly having accepted my decision, I handed it all over: the location, cake, menu, and yes, even the dress. Except, it's not a dress, it's the aforementioned suit that's on the tight side, and that I didn't see or try on until twelve hours before show time. What would I have done if it didn't fit? I have no idea. There was no plan B. I stuck my head in the sand and hoped for the best, and this is what I got.

We line up in two rows: Richard and I in the front and centre, the wedding guests surrounding us. Two down, my ex is standing there with his little daughter in his arms, my niece. In between us is my sister, his wife. Remember the theme of the day? Oh yes, it's awkward.

The rest of the day passes slowly. After the pictures, we file into the gorgeous dining room. It looks much more like a castle than the outside would suggest: whitewashed vaulted ceilings, wood beams, a pretty lace tablecloth and lace napkins on the table. We are served champagne, which is desperately needed. However, it being noon on a Monday, people only have one glass, which is far too little to create a festive atmosphere.

We sit down for lunch. The food is excellent: you can choose between 'halibut on a bed of fresh spinach, accompanied by porcini mushrooms and potato gratin,' or 'leg of hare à la mode in a prune sauce, accompanied by wine-soaked pear in a cranberry sauce, red cabbage (this is Germany, after all), steamed dumplings topped with buttery crumbs,' or 'pork medallions with a gorgonzola cheese crust, accompanied by pasta primavera and fresh seasonal vegetables.'

Conversation is halting. Our voices echo loudly in the stone-dining room, amplifying every word. It makes people self-conscious. The only thing worse than the intensified voices is when they die down, which happens frequently. Whenever the awkward silence descends, I desperately search for something to say. After all, it's our party, and I feel responsible for its success or failure. However, making small talk has never been my strength, and I usually have to suffer through it until someone else breaks the silence.

After lunch, we are at a loss for what to do next. We have to stick around for afternoon coffee, which will include the cutting of the cake. But how to fill the two hours in between? There's no music, no entertainment. We have exhausted our meager conversational skills.

In desperation, we decide to go for a walk. I'm wearing high heels, and I can't walk in them, but anything is better than to sit around the table for another minute. I teeter unsteadily down the steep hill in my cheap shoes, accompanied by my mother, aunt and grandmother. It's January and I'm freezing in my skimpy outfit, so after ten minutes or so we turn around to head back inside. Uncle Randy asks Richard and me if we want him to take some photos of the two of us, and we readily agree. That fills the rest of the lull, and by the time we are done, coffee is served.

By four o'clock, the torture is finally over. I'm sure our guests are as relieved as we are. We say our goodbyes, and then we ride back in my parents' car to my parents' house.

Richard and I plop down on my bed in my childhood room and turn to each other. Then, we both burst into laughter simultaneously.

"This was the worst wedding I have ever been to," I gasp, tears running down my cheeks.

Richard nods his head in agreement, unable to speak.

When he gets a hold of himself, he says, "You know how they say that rain on your wedding day is lucky? Let's make a new rule: the worse the wedding, the better the marriage."

"If that's true, we will have the world's best marriage!" I counter happily.

Looking at him, so handsome in his black suit and cowboy hat, bright blue eyes and the attractive silver beard, I finally feel like a bride, like I'm the luckiest girl in the world.

Chapter 1

SUCKER-PUNCHED

February 2001

I pull around the corner towards my parents' house. It's been eight weeks since I have been home, and I didn't want to come this weekend. But they insisted.

"We need you," they told me. "It's a family business, you are part of the family, you have to pull your weight."

I glower over the top of the steering wheel. I *hate* this small town. It's depressing the hell out of me, with its square stone buildings, nosey neighbours, and never-ending complaints of the locals. These people wouldn't know how to be happy if it hit them in the face. They enjoy being miserable. Well, guess what—so do I these days. I'll fit right in!

As I approach my parents' house, I suddenly see a car. *His* car. My heart starts to beat faster, my palms are getting moist, and I have butterflies in my stomach. He is here! At my house! I haven't seen him in three months, giving him the space he requested, despite it almost killing me. But the misery of the last three months is suddenly forgotten. He is here to tell me he is ready for a *real* relationship! That's why my parents insisted I come home! I'm so giddy with relief and excitement, I laugh out loud. I haphazardly park my car behind his, then pull down the visor and check my appearance in the little mirror. Damn, I look like a mess. No make-up, hair greasy and tied carelessly into a limp ponytail. *Shit.* I rummage in my purse for mascara or lip gloss, already knowing that I won't find any. I'm not the make-up carrying kind of girl, and over the last few months I have completely given up on my appearance. I wonder if I could manage to sneak into the house without them seeing me and take a quick shower? Almost immediately I dismiss the idea as impossible. Our dog will bark and give me away as soon as I open the door, and anyway, I'm way too impatient to see him. I yank out the elastic, brush my hair, and tie it up again more tidily. This will have to do.

After one last deep breath, I exit the car. My heart is beating so hard it almost hurts, and I wonder if this is what a heart attack feels like. No, it can't be. I'm only twenty-one, slightly overweight, but generally in good health.

I'm stalling, because suddenly I'm terrified to see him again. "Come on, you can do this," I encourage myself, and wipe my sweating palms on my jeans. I briefly close my eyes, and picture him: red hair, green eyes, crooked smile. Looking at me quizzically, like he is trying to figure out what I'm all about. Tall. He makes me feel small, which is important to me, since I feel huge most of the time. A broad grin spreads over my face, and with a burst of bravery I open the front door of our house and step into the hallway.

They are in the kitchen, as I knew they would be. Our entire life takes place in the huge, farm-style kitchen, with its tiled stove and the bench wrapping around it, the best place on cold winter nights. The large table seats eight people comfortably, not that we need it very often; we rarely have guests. But tonight, we do, and as our dog Roxy starts barking excitedly, I push open the door to greet her—and *him*.

For a moment, everything looks as expected. My dad is sitting in his usual chair, a glass of wine in front of him, his head turned towards me, with his customary hesitant smile on his lips. My mom sits across from him, smiling widely with too many teeth and, I notice in confusion, slightly hysterically. But I don't pause to wonder about it, because my eyes find *him*. He is sitting across the room, facing me, and my entire being floods with happiness. He has finally decided to come back to me! My broad grin starts to fade as I notice the expression on his face. He stares at me unsmilingly, with an expression I can't place right away. Anxious? Nervous? Sad? All those emotions are part of it, but the main one hits me a moment later right into my solar plexus, knocking the wind out of me: it's guilt. And as my eyes slowly trail to the left of him, I suddenly realize the source of his guilt in one horrible, excruciating moment: my sister. My younger sister Emma is sitting next to him, entirely too close, looking at me defiantly. As my gaze travels down, it comes to a screeching halt at their hands: they are clasped together. The boy I haven't been able to stop thinking about for *months*, my sort-of-boyfriend who was supposed to be my real boyfriend just as soon as he was ready, is holding *my sister's hand*.

The blood is rushing so loudly in my ears that I can't hear. I have no idea if anyone has said anything yet. Time has slowed down, burning this hideous moment into my brain for the rest of my life. While my eyes take in the terrible tableau in front of me, my brain has a difficult time catching up to what's happening.

"Wh-wh-what's going on?" I stutter, looking at him desperately. *Please,* please *have a simple explanation,* I implore him silently. His face is bright red, but he still hasn't said a word.

"Hello Miriam!" my mom says loudly, and I flinch. I have completely forgotten about my parents being in the same room. It seems that hours have passed since I first entered the kitchen, when it was less than a minute. I turn to face her, hoping for her to shed some light on the situation.

"What's going on?" I repeat, louder this time and without stuttering. "Why is he here? What are they doing?" My voice keeps rising in time with my rising agitation.

"Calm down," my mother says firmly, which is exactly the wrong thing to say. Has anyone ever calmed down when they were told to? No. It has the opposite effect, like pouring gasoline on a sweltering fire. I can feel hot tears stinging my eyes, and I explode.

"Why didn't you call me? What are you doing here in my house? AND WHY THE FUCK ARE YOU HOLDING MY SISTER'S HAND?" I scream at him. My mother opens her mouth in protest, and I turn on her. "Did you know about this? How long has this been going on? *Why didn't you tell me?"*

I turn on my heel and run out of the kitchen, up to my room, where I fall onto my bed and break down, sobbing uncontrollably.

Never in my life have I felt so betrayed. Such a fool. I'm more embarrassed and hurt than ever before. *How could they do this to me?*

Chapter 2
WONDER MAN

Five months earlier

"Miriam, can you do a delivery for me?" my mother yells from the other room.

"To whom?" I yell back, neither saying yes or no. I'm a reluctant contributor to the family business, a farm market/grocery-store. If it were up to me, I would have nothing to do with it, but unfortunately, it isn't. From the age of twelve I had to work every Saturday at the outdoor farm market, and pitch in wherever else they need me. Apparently, today it's delivering produce to one of the several restaurants we supply.

"We have a new customer," Mom says, walking into the kitchen. "He leased the little country restaurant in Niehau a while ago."

"Uh-hmm," I answer distractedly, continuing to flip through my magazine.

"He's a young guy, really nice. Your father has been talking to him quite a bit, he is very impressed by the young man," she continues, and that's when I look up and put the magazine away. My dad is a quiet, serious man, not known for his conversational skills. He hates idle chit-chat, and lives by the rule that if one has nothing of importance to say, one shouldn't say anything at all. For him to not only talk to someone, but be *impressed by* is high praise indeed.

"What's his story?" I ask.

"Well, he took over the restaurant six months ago," she tells me. "I think he wants to run a fine dining place, something a bit more special than what we have around here. But you know how people are, they won't jump on anything that's new and different. He's having a bit of a hard time getting customers through the door." I immediately sympathize with him. The people around here are suspicious by nature, and getting them to try something new is a nearly impossible task. He has his work cut out for him.

"Okay, I'll go," I say, jumping up. "What's his name?"

"Oliver."

We load up the truck, and I take off. I'm curious to meet this mysterious Oliver, who has captivated my parents.

The restaurant is less than ten minutes away. As I pull into the cobbled courtyard, I'm slightly nervous. I'm not good at meeting new people, always feeling awkward and getting tongue-tied quickly. But I'm here now, and I have a job to do. As I'm getting out of the delivery truck, he comes out of the house.

Wearing chef-whites, he walks towards me with a friendly smile. Oliver is tall, at least six feet, with broad shoulders and a narrow waist. He has red hair, green eyes, and a contagious crooked grin. "Hi!" he greets me. "Let me help you."

"I'm Miriam," I introduce myself. "My parents are the Meiers, and they asked me to deliver your produce today."

"I figured," he grins at me. "I know the truck. I'm Oliver." He deftly takes two boxes of lettuce from the back and leads me to his walk-in refrigerator. I follow with the peppers and cucumbers.

"How come I haven't seen you before?" he calls over his shoulder.

"I'm at college," I explain. "I study Forestry in Munich."

"Really? That's awesome!" He puts down the boxes, and looks at me more carefully. "Forestry, huh? So, you are going to walk around with a green hat and a rifle once you are done?"

"Yup, that's the plan. A gun, my dog, and my jeep."

His face brightens. "You like dogs?"

"*Love* them," I enthuse. "Having my dog with me all day is half the reason why I went into Forestry in the first place!"

"Well, let me introduce you to Freddy then."

"Is Freddy your dog?" I guess.

"Yeah. He is up in my apartment. I can't have him walk around freely because he has some issues. I got him from the pound, and they told me that he was abused by his previous owner."

My heart goes out to him. Freddy, that is. But I also look at Oliver with new eyes. Not only is he a nice and attractive guy, but he also loves animals.

"I would love to meet him."

I spend two hours there. Oliver lets Freddy out, a Rottweiler/German Shepherd mix, who takes a shine to me. The feeling is mutual; I can't get enough of him. He is beautiful, clingy, and damaged, and almost pathetically grateful for attention. I scratch his ears, hug and kiss him, and coo to him in my special dog-voice, telling him what a good boy he is.

Oliver shows me the restaurant: a gorgeous dining room that looks like a medieval grotto with stone walls, arched ceilings, and fresh flowers on each table; his little office that overlooks the cobble-stoned courtyard; and the kitchen, "where I spend my life," as he puts it.

Oliver offers me a drink, and I happily accept. He makes me a cappuccino, pours himself a cup of black coffee, and tells me about himself. At only twenty-three years old, he has already worked several years at a hotel, owned a bistro for a while, and lived and worked in Paris for six months.

"But this is my dream," he tells me, gesturing around him. "Owning my own restaurant, bringing Parisian fine dining to the country."

"That's so wonderful!" I exclaim, looking at him admiringly.

"You want to come by tonight?" he asks after glancing at his watch. "I have to start prepping, but I want you to try my food. What do you say?"

"I'd love to!"

On the drive home, I can't wipe the silly grin from my face. I have a date for tonight! Oliver is a great guy, and so interesting. I can't wait to see him again.

As I walk through the door of my parents' store, my mother notices my dreamy expression. "You look happy," she states, looking at me questioningly.

"I am! Oh, Mom, Oliver is so nice, we had a wonderful time! And he invited me for dinner tonight, he wants to cook for me!" I tell her eagerly.

Her face lights up. "Really? That's great! Tell me more."

And I do. For the first time in years, we have the kind of mother-daughter chat you see in movies, where mother and daughter are best friends and share everything. It's a real Gilmore Girls-moment—and it is *lightyears* away from our usual routine. When I was a child, and eager to please, we had an easy relationship, but as soon as I developed my own mind as a teenager, we butted heads at every opportunity. We haven't had a close heart-to-heart in *years*. We try to understand the other person, but we are mystified by each other.

To share a rare moment of mutual understanding is precious. I treasure this rare connection we have much more than the actual visit with the guy.

My mother and I are opposites: I'm an emotional and sensitive person who wants to talk about her feelings excessively, cry openly, be cuddled and hugged and reassured repeatedly that she is loved, even when screwing up.

My mother doesn't care for this trait of mine. She is the kind of person who keeps her feelings hidden deep inside her, and doesn't want anyone—not even her children—to see them. Open displays of affection are not her style. When pressed, she once told me that, "you know how I feel about you, why do you want to hear it all the time?"

(Because I'm needy. I didn't choose to be this way, but somehow ended up with an extra dose of neediness and insecurity. It's at least as frustrating to me as it is to my mom.)

If she were to play a character in a movie, she would portray the tough, cold Russian spy, while I'm the overly emotional, gushy, touchy-feely Disney princess. Minus the hair and glamorous clothes.

She is a highly private person and believes that self-doubt, insecurities, and feelings should stay tucked safely away from the prying eye of the public.

I have the powerful urge to share my doubts and weaknesses, to feel less alone. I believe that sharing them will make me stronger. She believes that it will make one look weaker.

To make a long story short: our approaches to life couldn't be more different.

But I'm just a person (and an above average insecure one at that), and

I crave her approval. Closely followed by resenting everything she stands for and wants to teach me.

As you can imagine, the past few years have been a battle ground, and we are both raw and bruised from it. Our relationship is fragile, always on the verge of the next fight.

Sharing a moment of mutual understanding and genuine joy is rare and precious beyond words. I'm so happy about it, my excitement about meeting Oliver pales in comparison.

Nevertheless, I have a date (it *is* a date, right? I'm not completely sure about that), and that beats my original plans of staying home and watching TV. What to wear? That's the big question. One of the problems I'm having is that most of my clothes are in my apartment three hours away from my parents' house. I'm only home for the weekend, and all I have brought with me are jeans and nondescript sweaters. But even if I would have all my clothes with me, the other problem is that I have gained some considerable weight over the last couple of years, which means that most of my clothes don't fit. I hate to buy a bigger size, instead squeezing myself into clothes two or three sizes too small, making me look and feel like a sausage. The few items that I have reluctantly bought in the right size are plain and unexciting, because I also happen to be in a major style crisis.

There is only one solution: I need to go shopping. A quick look at my watch tells me that I have enough time to squeeze in a quick trip to the mall before tonight's date to buy something half-decent.

At 7 o'clock that night I'm ready. I look at myself in the mirror, trying to see myself with Oliver's eyes: shoulder-length hair, dyed auburn, framing a round face prone to break-outs (thankfully none tonight, what a miracle!). I'm dressed in an entirely new outfit: dark boot-cut jeans with enough stretch to make them feel comfortable, and a simple black top, low-cut to show off some cleavage. I plan on leaving my jacket on to hide my arms, because I hate their chunkiness. I don't like what I see, but there is nothing I can do about it now. I promise myself to go on a diet tomorrow, sigh, and turn away from my reflection.

"I'm leaving!" I yell to my parents, and they call back to have fun, and remind me that I have to get up early tomorrow.

During the ten-minute drive to his place, the butterflies in my stomach go wild. The last real date I have been on was when I was fourteen years old, with a boy from my class. I was so terrified of going that I took my best friend along. Romantic, no? We went to a movie and had ice cream after, and I didn't say a single word to him the entire time. My friend did all the talking, and I sat there, mortified, not knowing what to say. Since then I've had relationships, but every single one has started out with us being friends first. Dating is something I am neither familiar nor comfortable with.

Before I know it, I arrive at the restaurant. "Well, you got this far," I mutter to myself, quickly jumping out of the car and heading to the door, before I can change my mind.

I don't know what to expect, but it certainly isn't this. Instead of a bustling, busy restaurant thronged with people, I step into a silent room. All the tables are empty. The lone waitress is perched behind the bar, flipping through a magazine, looking bored. At the sound of the door opening, she looks up hopefully. "Good evening!" she greets me pleasantly. "For one?"

"Uhm, no," I stammer, turning red. "I'm looking for Oliver?"

"He's in the kitchen," she says, pointing behind her and returning to her magazine.

I walk the short distance to the kitchen, where I find Oliver sitting on a stool, smoking and staring into space.

"Hey!" I say softly, and he turns towards me, a smile spreading across his face.

"Miriam, you came!" he says, and I nod, smiling back.

"What's going on outside?" I ask him, gesturing towards the dining room. "The dining room is empty. Are you closed today?"

He looks away, blowing a smoke ring into the air. "Nope," he says. "It's a slow night."

Then, in an obvious effort to change the subject, "Are you hungry?"

I'm not. I'm nervous and off my game, and the last thing I want to do is eat. Besides, I don't know how to handle myself. Should I eat just a tiny amount, to demonstrate my ladylike self-restraint? Or is it more attractive to dig in, demolish a huge plate-full, to demonstrate my un-diva-like behaviour? I have read that guys like that, but I suspect they only do with skinny girls. If skinny girls eat a lot, they are regarded as super-cool, uncomplicated chicks. If chubby girls do the same, everybody is looking at them as pigs. Life isn't fair.

I decide it's safer to decline for now. "Not really," I tell him. "Maybe later?"

"You want a drink?" he offers next. Now we're talking.

"Yes, please!" I reply gratefully. Just what I need to take the edge off. He gets up and walks outside to the bar, and I follow behind.

"Hey Rosie, could you get me a beer?" he asks the waitress. Then he turns to me. "What would you like?"

"I'll have a beer as well." Not knowing what to do with myself, I start wandering around the dining room. Oliver leans against the counter, lights another cigarette, and chats to the waitress, Rosie.

"Your beer," she calls out to me a moment later. I return to the bar, take the proffered glass from her, and take a sip. There is silence for a moment. God, this is awkward. I simply can't think of anything to say.

Rosie doesn't have that problem. She starts asking me about myself, teasing Oliver, and chatting about village gossip and whatever else pops into her head. It's my first date all over again. I suck at this!

An hour later, Oliver's neighbours drop in, and I know that the so-called 'date' is over. However, they are entertaining, and we laugh, drink and talk for hours. When I leave shortly after midnight, I'm grinning from ear to ear, because even though as a date, the evening was a disaster, it was still fun.

To my delight, Oliver keeps inviting me back over the next few weeks. Friday nights become a weekly ritual, and I look forward to them more with each passing week. We usually hang out at the restaurant, with an assortment of different people around, chatting, eating, and drinking. He is interested in my family, asking endless questions about our store, my parents, and what it was like growing up in a family business. I'm flattered by so much interest in, what I consider, a boring upbringing, and tell my parents all about it. They are *thrilled*. With one daughter learning the trade of being a goldsmith, and the other one studying Forestry, my parents have resigned themselves to the fact that the business will die with them. Despite assuring us that we can do whatever we want with our lives and never pressuring us into taking over the business, knowing that we aren't interested must have hurt them more than I realized. Having someone outside the family show so much admiration gives them fresh energy and pride.

And who gets the credit for that energy and pride? Me! Well, Oliver does, but it is because of *my* friendship with him. The glow of my parents' approval elevates our relationship to formerly unknown heights. Suddenly, we are close. I haven't told them details about my life in years, fearing my mother's disapproval and her power to say no to my choices.

But all this is different now. I tell her everything Oliver and I talk about, and she couldn't be happier and more approving of our friendship. Several times she asks if there is a future relationship in the works, but I have since learnt that he has a girlfriend. Oliver didn't mention her until our third Friday night, and even though I should be mad about him skipping this rather important part of his life, I'm secretly relieved. So *that's* the reason why our friendship hasn't progressed to the next level! I'm sure the spark between us is real and not just in my imagination. She lives and works in a different town, and they haven't seen each other in weeks. Oliver assures me that the relationship is over, that he doesn't love her anymore; he just hasn't gotten the courage to break up with her yet. I think he is waiting for her to do the breaking up.

Since we first met I have developed a serious crush on him, less because I like him and more because I have the full approval of my parents for the first time in my adult life. Oliver has managed to fix our strained relationship, he makes us all feel prouder of our family business, and he is great company. He is like wonder woman with a penis!

And it's about to get even better.

(Closely followed by getting worse. A LOT. But luckily, I don't know that yet.)

"Hey, can you come over? Right now? Something happened."

The phone call comes only minutes after I have arrived at my parents' house. "Sure!" I exclaim, worried. "What's going on? Are you all right?"

"I did it!" Oliver says, his voice wobbling slightly. "I broke up with Susie."

"What? Your girlfriend?"

"Yup. And I need to see you. Can you come?"

"I'm on my way."

I grab my coat and purse and fly out of the house. My heart is singing—he has broken up with his long-time girlfriend! He is free! And he wants to see me! This can only mean one thing: we are about to start a relationship.

I drive to his place in record time and run into the house. Oliver is sitting behind the desk in his office, staring out of the window, eerily still. When he turns to me, his eyes are red and he looks miserable. Wordlessly I go to him, take him into my arms, and let him cry.

"It was awful," he whispers into my hair. "I thought she felt the same way about us, but she didn't. She said she had given me space because of the restaurant, because she didn't want to distract me. I guess I told her that I need to focus all my energy on the business until it takes off, but that was just an excuse! I thought she was as relieved as I was that we didn't have to pretend any more. Oh God, she was so devastated. I think she will never forgive me."

I listen, rocking him gently, making soothing noises and rubbing his back.

"Of course she will," I assure him. "Break-ups are horrendous. Once she's had time to digest it, she will realize that your relationship was over a long time ago. It's the best for both of you."

I lean back and look fiercely into his eyes.

"Listen to me, Oliver. You are a good man. Sometimes we have to make painful decisions in life. It hurts now, but it's kinder than dragging on a relationship that doesn't make you happy any more. Sooner or later it would have ended anyway, but with even more pain and hate. You did a good thing."

Oliver stares back at me, desperate to believe my words. Then he puts his hand on the back of my head, and slowly pulls me closer. I automatically close my eyes and hold my breath. Is he going to kiss me?

A moment later, our lips touch. The kiss starts out hesitantly, our noses bumping clumsily, his stubble rubbing my chin. He tastes of cigarettes and salty tears, of hurt and longing. I pull him closer, wanting to give him all the comfort I can. He clings to me tightly, like a man who is drowning.

I move into his apartment the same night. Oliver asks me if I could stay the night, and of course I say yes. How could I not? He needs me, and I'm thrilled that he chose me to be by his side during this difficult time. I still don't know exactly what is going on between us, if it is a friendship with benefits-thing, a budding romance, or the beginning of the rest of our lives together. For the moment, I push the question aside, deciding that I will deal with it later. I go home to pack a few things, and tell my delighted mother that I will stay at Oliver's. She couldn't be more excited, and sends me off with a rare hug and a conspiratorial "Good luck."

For the next eight days, I put my regular life on hold.

I blow off school, my friends, my job. All I want is to be there for him, to get to know him better. We spend our days making elaborate plans for the future, about us running the restaurant together, and combining his and my family's businesses. Never before have I considered to take over my parents' store, but suddenly, the idea doesn't seem so crazy. Maybe that is my destiny after all?

I hang out in the kitchen with him when he cooks and help serve the few guests that come in. When he is busy, I take his dog Freddy for long walks, dreaming of a future where we will work side by side, co-owning a successful business, amongst the leading members of the community. We will work hard but also play hard with our large circle of friends, who drop in spontaneously and often, and life will be full and rich and wonderful.

At night, we make passionate and slightly desperate love, which leaves me lying there long after he has fallen asleep, staring into the darkness, wondering what the hell I am doing. The nights are the only time where I can't escape the truth: this isn't me. This isn't my life. I barely know Oliver, who is an enigma, despite us spending every minute together. We seem to be speaking different languages, unable to communicate with each other.

He is a mystery, with many secrets, and it drives me nuts and keeps me captivated in equal measures. I desperately want to get to know him, to be able to glean an insight into his mind and his heart. But despite him talking, and me listening, I have no idea who he is. I get the distinct sense that he is putting up a wall, hiding behind it, and I can't penetrate that wall.

But for now, I eagerly gobble up every crumb he throws my way. He is putting me into *his* dream, assigning me a role for *his* version of a perfect future, and I am flattered by that. I don't realize at the time that it isn't about *me*, or *us*—it is about himself. I have so little idea about what *I* want that I am quite happy to have someone else make that decision for me. Not only happy, but grateful. He is saving me from myself.

Our arrangement is built on a relationship that has just fallen apart after four years, an insecure girl who is desperate for the approval of others, and the mutual desire to start afresh. We are both stuck in lives we don't like, and we are looking for an escape. We think we have found it with each other, but it will dawn on both of us that we haven't.

The only problem is: it doesn't dawn on us at the same time. (These things rarely do.)

On day eight, it collapses.

I have been feeling morose all day. There is a weird undercurrent between us, and we keep our distance, Oliver puttering around in the kitchen, me hiding in his unfinished living room, listening to music, smoking, and brooding.

Eventually he joins me, sitting down on the floor opposite of me. I avoid his gaze, feeling raw and unbalanced and close to tears.

"What are you doing?" he asks after a while.

"What are *we* doing?" I counter, voice wobbling.

"What is this, Oliver? This weird thing we have going on? I don't know if we are in a relationship, or just sleeping together. What are we doing?" I repeat, tears in my eyes.

"I don't know," he whispers. We look at each other miserably.

"I think I should go," I finally say, willing him to tell me to stay.

He doesn't. "I think that's probably for the best," Oliver says instead, and I see a flicker of relief cross his face. "I need some time to think, to get over my break-up with Susie. I'll call you, okay?"

He leans forward to give me a kiss, but I pull away, hurt. "Okay then,"

I say as flippantly as I can manage, and get up with some difficulty, my legs cramping from sitting cross-legged on the floor for so long. "See ya," I call over my shoulder, limping out of the room towards the bedroom to get my stuff. Why couldn't I walk away more gracefully? I berate myself, focusing on this one detail, so I won't have to face what just happened. I couldn't have looked more awkward and clumsy. Damn it! I throw my clothes carelessly into my bag, then storm into the bathroom to grab my washbag, flinging my toiletries into it with unnecessary force. After a moment's deliberation, I take my toothbrush out again and place it back into the cup, next to Oliver's. "Just a little reminder that I was here," I say aloud. Back in the bedroom, I hesitate, wondering if I should leave one of my panties behind for the same reason. I decide against it, unwilling to remind him of my size 14 ass.

Looking around for a moment, I wonder when I will see this room again. I'm sure it is only a matter of time, a question of when, not if.

Not for a moment does it occur to me that this is the last time I will ever see it again.

Chapter 3
"ON A BREAK"

At first, I'm not too worried. I'm sure that Oliver will call, that he really just needs a bit of time. At twenty, I'm naïve and trusting, never really having had a negative experience with boys before. My two previous boyfriends have both been long-term relationships, and when they ended I was sad, but not heartbroken.

I'm even relieved to return to my normal life, having been seriously unsettled by this bizarre week I spent so far removed from reality. But after three days, I'm getting worried. Surely, he must have had enough time by now? I discuss it with my roommate Amber, asking her advice.

"Should I call him?" I ask her over glasses of wine on the third evening.

"Absolutely not," she tells me firmly. "He wants time, give him time. Let him miss you. Guys like the chase, they don't like clingy girls."

Amber has some experience in this matter, being in a tumultuous relationship with a freedom-loving guy who will regularly disappear for days at a time, to "clear his head."

"I hate this," I whine, refilling my glass for the fourth time. "Why do we have to play these games? Isn't it childish? We live in the 21st century for God's sake, can't I just be an independent woman and pick up the phone myself?"

"Independent and running after a guy?" Amber states drily. "A bit of a contradiction, don't you think?"

"But I miss him," I insist, slurring my words slightly. "And I'm sure he misses me too. He's hurting after his break-up, he needs someone to comfort him. He needs *me*," I add hastily, seeing Amber opening her mouth, no doubt to say something sarcastic.

"Don't call him," she says firmly. "Trust me on this."

I listen to her that night. But the next day, I go to the drug store after school and buy Oliver's aftershave, Hugo Boss, which lays the foundation for an unhealthy nightly ritual. Every evening I retreat into my room, curl up on my cheap, lumpy futon, and listen to heartbreak-music, while simultaneously sniffing the aftershave bottle to remind myself of Oliver. While Dolores O'Riordan from *The Cranberries* croons 'Zombie', I noisily sob into my pillow.

Occasionally I call Oliver, which are bizarre conversations consisting of meaningless small talk, usually involving his dog Freddy, how the restaurant is doing, or what he and my dad have talked about. He never asks anything about me. I take my cue from him, trying to keep those phone calls lighthearted, but they devastate me. In my head, I'm screaming at him: "Did you have enough time yet? Do you miss me? Are we together?" But I don't dare bring it up.

Oliver never calls me, and after a while, I stop calling him. It's just too hard.

I also regularly talk to my mom during that time, an unusual occurrence in our complicated relationship, asking her what to do about the Oliver situation. In the beginning, she encourages me to not give up, to give him the space he requests, while gently reminding him that there is a new, better woman (me) waiting for him.

"Guys are simple," she says confidently. "You can manipulate them without them realizing it. Let him know that you are the right woman for him by listening to him, being supportive, offering your help. Don't be needy, and for God's sake, don't talk about your feelings all the time like you tend to do." I bristle at those words, offended.

"I don't talk about my feelings all the time!" I protest automatically, even though I suspect I do.

But it doesn't matter anyway. By this point, he and I have stopped talking.

I have also stopped calling my mom, annoyed with her. Instead, I indulge in my ritual of listening to sad music, compulsively sniffing Hugo Boss like it's my job, crying, and eating copious amounts of soft pretzels and chocolate (my comfort foods) with renewed vigor. It's now November, my least favourite month of the year, and it is the ideal setting for an extended pity party.

I'm miserable. At the time, I don't know it, but years later I will recognize that I wasn't pining for Oliver, the man; I was pining for Oliver, the *idea*. I wanted a man who could fix the complicated relationship with my parents; who could tell me what would make me happy; and who would love me passionately for the rest of my life. *A tall order.*

I thought I was grieving for a missed chance at love. Well, I was. But, even more than that, I was grieving for the loss of friendship I had with my parents. For a brief, blissful time in our lives, we had been the perfect family: united by the same goal, invigorated by someone who admired us as a family and a business, we had been closer than ever before.

With Oliver gone from my life (temporarily? I *so* hope it is temporary), so is the intimacy my parents and I have enjoyed during that short amount of time.

Christmas is a depressing affair that year. I go home as usual, but I'm not exactly feeling the Christmas spirit. I'm hurting, I have gained ten pounds, and I'm still secretly hoping that Oliver will make a grand gesture, which involves showing up at our house and declaring his undying love for me. I know that this is a most unlikely scenario, but a lifetime of romantic books and movies have instilled an unshakable belief in the power of love in me. I despise myself for it, but still, I can't help it—I'm hoping he will come around. However, with every passing day where he doesn't show up, it becomes clearer that he hasn't come around, which doesn't improve my mood.

To add insult to injury, my younger sister Emma, who was a chubby child and teenager, has gone through a break-up herself and lost a staggering amount of weight in the process. For the first time in our lives she is skinnier than me, and I take great offense by that.

"How did you do it?" I ask her, more aggressively than strictly necessary.

"Less calories in than out," she replies snippily, lighting another cigarette. She looks pale and gaunt and is smoking like a fiend. I should be worried about her, but I have my own problems.

Our relationship isn't always easy. From the moment she was born, I was worried that she may take up too much of our parents' love. I was an insecure, needy child, while Emma was independent and self-sufficient. I was afraid that she was easier to love, because she required so much less attention than I did. Emma, in turn, was a typical younger child, wanting to do everything I did, and following me around like a puppy. We fought often and ferociously, hitting and biting and pinching each other, but when we didn't fight, we had the best time together; we could just look at each other and crack up, laughing until our bellies hurt, while our friends looked on bewildered, not getting it.

As we entered our teenage years, our usually antagonistic relationship went through several amicable, surprisingly long stretches of peace. During those happy times, we made big plans, Emma wanting to become a photographer, and me hoping to be a journalist. We dreamed of moving to New York City together, sharing a tiny apartment, working for the same magazine. Considering that none of us spoke a lick of English, that we had never been anywhere but the countries immediately surrounding Germany, and that neither she nor I had any formal training in our chosen professions, our chances of making it were slim (to put it mildly). To nobody's surprise, this dream popped like a soap bubble.

Emma started an apprenticeship as a goldsmith and moved away to live with our aunt and uncle. I was at a loss for what to do after high school. If I could have, I would have liked to take a year off school, to work and figure out what I wanted to do with my life. But my parents were adamant that I go to college, and in a moment of recklessness, I signed up for Forestry.

I should probably also mention that I was in the grip of a serious bout of (undiagnosed) depression, which always manifests itself in me wanting to hide away from the world. What is it that people say? Never reply when you're angry, never make a promise when you're happy, and never make a decision when you're sad? Yeah, I should have listened to that.

I made the decision to spend the rest of my life in the forest when I was the saddest I had ever been, and unsurprisingly, it came back to bite me in the ass. But more about that later.

On the last night of our Christmas vacation, Emma and I sit around the kitchen table, bored. Our parents are watching a movie, but neither of us feels like joining them.

"Do you want to go for a walk?" I ask Emma, itching to get out of the house for a bit.

"Sure," she answers, and we pack some provisions before heading out: our Christmas cigarettes (cigarettes flavoured with oranges, cloves, and cinnamon, that leave a delicious taste on your lips) and a thermos filled with hot mulled wine.

It's a cold, clear night. We trudge through the snow in companionable silence, our dog Roxy scampering happily in front of us, darting in and out of people's driveways. We are headed towards the old sawmill, where we have hung out frequently when we were younger.

Once there, we sit down on a pile of wood, I pour us some mulled wine, and we pass the cup back and forth between us.

"How *are* you?" I ask my younger sister eventually. "You really lost a lot of weight, and you're white as a ghost. Are you okay? Is it because of Harry?" Harry is her ex. They had been together for two years, and their relationship was very strange: they started to dress alike, in faded jeans and chunky fisherman's sweaters, both painting their nails black, and having the same hairstyle. They made themselves look like twins, and it was *weird*. Emma and I drifted apart during her time with Harry, because I thought she had lost her mind.

"No, not really," Emma answers, blowing a perfect smoke ring into the air and watching it drift away. "It's not that I really miss him, just that it's strange not having him in my life any more. It's like there is a big hole in my life, and I don't know how to fill it."

"You did spend a lot of time together," I confirm, careful not to say anything negative about the relationship. It's over, no point rehashing what I'd thought about it.

"What do you want to do next? Any plans?"

Emma shakes her head. "Nope, no clue. Concentrating on work, I guess." She stares down into her lap for a moment, then she visibly shakes herself, as if wanting to rid herself of a bad memory.

"So, what about you? What got you so down?" I gawk at her for a moment, speechless.

"Don't you know?"

She looks back at me, shaking her head. "Know what?"

I can't believe it. How can my only sister not know that my world has crumpled around me? It seems unreal. Then again, I haven't told her. I assumed our mother had kept her up to date, but I guess she hasn't.

I take a deep breath, and tell her a somewhat censored version (I leave out the embarrassing parts) of Oliver's and my brief, yet intense love affair. Or whatever it is—I still don't know what to call it. In telling her, I simply refer to it as "this thing we had."

When I'm done, there is a brief silence. Then we both burst into laughter simultaneously.

"Is there anyone more pathetic than the two of us?" I giggle.

"The unlucky-in-love sisters," Emma cries, clutching her stomach.

"We are such losers!" I howl, and we both dissolve into a fresh onslaught of laughter.

It takes us a long time to recover enough to be able to get up and make our way home. My mood has improved drastically, and I feel cleansed and pleasantly drowsy after our laughing fit. Before we go inside the house, I turn to Emma, put my arm around her and say, jokingly, "Just promise me one thing: don't go after Oliver. Okay?"

Chapter 4

BETRAYAL

The present

It's the middle of the night. I can't sleep, my eyes are swollen and puffy from hours of crying, and the thought of having to get up for work in a couple of hours turns my stomach. I still can't believe what happened last night. Oliver and Emma? Together? And my parents knew about it and didn't tell me? The magnitude of the betrayal is so immense, I can't wrap my head around it. Every time I try to grasp what they have done, my brain shuts down. It's all too much. My heart beats so fast, I'm worried I might get a panic attack. I feel so lonely that I'm physically hurting. The loneliness is sinking her teeth into me, paralyzing me with fear. What am I going to do now? How can I recover from this?

Earlier that evening, my mother knocked on the door, wanting to come in and "explain."

"Go away," I shrieked, not wanting to see anyone. Despite my protests, she came in anyway. Typical.

I turned my head towards the wall, refusing to look at her. When she sat down next to me on the bed, I pulled my pillow over my head, demonstrating how much I didn't want to listen to her.

Unsurprisingly, she started to speak anyway. She told me that while Oliver put on a brave face to the world, he was in deep trouble. His business was losing money daily and he didn't know what to do. My parents had developed a friendship with him, and he was asking them for advice. They invited him for dinner a few times. My sister, who had moved back home after her break-up, was there. They struck up a friendship. One thing led to another.

"But what about me?" I interrupted. "Didn't you even consider how this would affect me? Any of you?"

"What you had was a fling," she said, waving one hand dismissively. "You two are way too different, it would have never worked."

I was shocked into silence. How could my own mother disregard my feelings like they were nothing? Didn't she know me at all?

Having said what she came to say, she got up and walked towards the door. Before she left, she turned around and gave me one last piece of advice: "Pull yourself together, Miriam. Things happen for a reason. You will see, it's better this way."

Now, hours later, I stare up at the ceiling, wondering what to do. What do you do if you have hit rock bottom? I have nobody left in the world. No boyfriend, no family. *I'm all alone.* Deep down I'm dimly aware that this is overly dramatic, but I can't help it—that's how I feel. Should I run away? I could go back to my own apartment, three hours away from them all. It would serve them right. Maybe then they would realize what they have done to me? But almost immediately, I dismiss the idea. I came home because they need me in the store, and my parents are paying the rent for my apartment. I owe them. Leaving them hanging isn't a good idea.

Shortly before dawn, I finally fall into a fitful sleep, only to be awoken by my alarm an hour later.

The face that stares back at me from the mirror looks like something straight out of a horror movie. My eyes are almost swollen shut from all the crying. My skin is red and blotchy, with two fresh pimples sprouting on my chin. I literally take a step back, dismayed. I can't go out into the world looking like this! I tentatively step closer to the sink again, and splash cold water in my face for a minute. It feels good, but looking back up, I see that it barely made a difference to my appearance. What should I do about my eyes? Cucumber slices? Ice cubes? Tea bags? One of these is supposed to help with swelling, but I can't remember which one. In the end, I settle on a cold washcloth, because I'm not yet ready to leave the safety of my bedroom. I cover my eyes with the washcloth and lie back down, considering my next move.

The most pressing task is getting through the day. I will have to face my parents and my sister, and I'm determined not to apologize, and even more importantly, not to cry. I sincerely hope that Oliver has at least enough decency to stay away from our house today. I simply can't deal with him.

After a few minutes, I take the washcloth off my face and check the swelling. I still look like a gargoyle, but it's gone down a bit. Next step:

make-up. Since I didn't bring any, I raid my mother's make-up bag. I slather on the foundation, trying to hide the dark circles under my eyes and the two humongous pimples on my chin. Checking in the mirror, I see that I'm only semi-successful. I add another layer of foundation, and seal it all in with powder. She doesn't have any blush, so I look ghostly white, but there's nothing I can do about it. I experimentally pinch my cheeks, like the heroine of a Victorian novel, but it doesn't do the trick. Too much foundation, probably. To finish my face off I add some eye shadow and mascara, and then I'm done. I won't win any beauty contests today, but at least my face is one colour now. The dark shadows, red pimples, and blotchiness are all concealed under a thick layer of foundation that's not exactly my skin colour, but once I've put on a turtle neck sweater to hide the real colour of my neck, nobody will notice.

I take a deep breath, trying to steel myself, and then I walk into the kitchen. My dad is there, eating a slice of toast and drinking coffee.

"Morning," I mumble, not looking at him.

"Morning," he replies, and then hesitates. I glance at him and see him struggling, clearly debating whether he should continue speaking. In typical dad fashion, he closes his mouth again and says nothing.

I pour myself a cup of coffee, and lean against the kitchen counter, not trusting my fragile composure to hold it together if I sit down with him.

"It's cold today," he ventures after a minute of uncomfortable silence. "Did you bring your warm winter coat?"

"How could you not tell me?" I burst out suddenly, and to my horror, my eyes fill with tears. "I was so humiliated last night! You *know* that Oliver and I were together, and I thought we were just on a break, because he needed time, but that we would get back together. I've been waiting and waiting for him, and meanwhile, he has become part of the family and hooking up with Emma, and you all knew and *nobody told me*!"

I'm fully crying now, and Dad looks at me unhappily. We have always been close, and seeing me like this upsets him. Also, he's uncomfortable with too many emotions, and seems at a loss at what to do with me.

"We didn't think it was serious between you two," he says eventually. "You've barely come home, and you and Oliver haven't seen each other in months, right?"

"I know," I sob. "But it wasn't my idea, it was Oliver's. He wanted a break to figure things out, but we never broke up. I tried to talk to him in the beginning, but he was so weird that I stopped calling him. But Mom knew about all this! I told her! It feels like she replaced me with him, because he's more useful to her."

"Miriam, you know that's not true," Dad says helplessly. "I think she wanted to wait and see if anything would actually happen between Oliver and Emma. You should talk to her about it, she can explain it better than I can."

"Ugh, no thank you, I heard her explanation last night. 'Poor Oliver has so many problems, he needs our help. And if that means that we betray our own daughter, oh well, too bad so sad.'" I say nastily, feeling immediately even worse.

"Sorry," I mutter, not really meaning it.

Dad looks at his watch and then gets up. "Well, we have to get started," he says, putting his plate and coffee cup into the sink. Looking at my tear-smeared face, he asks tentatively, "Are you going to be okay?"

"Nope," I reply, but then say sarcastically, "but no worries, I'll come to work. The show must go on." Without waiting for an answer, I stomp out of the room.

I know that I'm behaving like a bitch, but I can't help it. I want to hurt them as much as they have hurt me. The usual coping mechanism for problems in my family is to ignore them, to not talk about it. Focus on work, get your chores done, and don't obsess about feelings. Particularly self-indulgent, self-pitying feelings. My parents can't stand self-pity.

But I'm not practical like that. I let my emotions sweep me up and take me away, on wild roller coaster rides of exhilarating highs and devastating lows. Once they start building up inside of me, they slowly rise to the surface like ever-expanding bubbles, and I'm powerless to stop them. If I try to keep me feelings inside, I will surely choke. How can you stop that? Where is the off switch? I can't seem to find it.

This despair I'm feeling is so heavy, I'm afraid it will pull me down and drown me.

The store is busy, which is good. I'm serving customers, getting more produce when we run low, even talking to people when it's unavoidable. But my head feels like it's packed in cotton, and I'm going through the motions like a sleepwalker. I have no idea what I'm telling people, or if I give them the right order. My only focus is to get to the end of the day. I avoid talking to my parents, only asking them work-related questions. Luckily Emma isn't there, she is at her own work, so I don't have to deal with her.

After the longest work day of my life, we are finally done. I practically run to my parents' house, throw the few things I brought in my bag, and say a curt goodbye. There is no way I'm sticking around.

I cry the entire ride home, all three hours of it. When I arrive at my apartment, I'm numb with exhaustion. Amber is out, which suits me fine because I don't have the energy to talk. I drop my bag on the floor, and go straight to bed, pulling the covers over my head. I want to hide from the world.

I fall asleep almost instantly. But my sleep is filled with nightmares, and I wake up with a start a few hours later, soaked with sweat and wild-eyed. For a moment, I think it was all just a nightmare, and I'm overcome with sweet relief—until I remember. Oliver and Emma, sitting next to each other, hand in hand. My parents knowing. Me walking in with that foolish, hopeful smile, thinking he came to see me. The humiliation.

"Oh God," I groan out loud. "What am I going to do?"

I stay in bed for two days, eating Nutella straight from the jar, followed by cereal straight from the box, feeling miserable. On the third day, Amber marches into my room, a determined look on her face.

"Okay missy, I gave you your time to feel sorry for yourself, but enough is enough. Let's get you into the shower, I'll clean up the room and then we go out for breakfast and talk, okay?" It's not a question, it's a command. I half-heartedly try to protest, but she is having none of it.

"Chop, chop, up you go," she says, pulling my covers off me.

"Hey, it's cold!" I whine.

"It's nice and warm in the shower," Amber says briskly, opening the window wide. I give up and slink into the bathroom.

The shower does make me feel marginally better. Stepping outside into the weak winter sunshine, I blink and shield my eyes. I haven't stepped foot outside in three days, which is unheard of for me—I'm usually out in nature every single day, craving fresh air and light. Amber bundles me into her car, and drives us to our favourite coffee shop. I haven't said a single word, but she doesn't seem to expect anything. Once she's ordered a Latte Macchiato and a chocolate croissant for each of us, she turns and eyes me kindly.

"What exactly are you so upset about?" she asks me, putting her hand on mine.

My eyes automatically fill with tears, and I tell her what happened at home.

"Oh sweetie, I'm so sorry," she says once I'm done. "That's tough. Who are you most upset about? Your sister, your parents, or Oliver?"

I think about the question carefully, while chewing on my croissant. My first impulse is to say Oliver—that bastard!—but on second thought it's really Emma and our mother. I told both how I felt about Oliver, and they not only ignored my feelings, but trampled all over them and lied about it. Well, not lied, but didn't tell me, which is a lie by omission.

"You know," I start slowly, trying to put my confusing thoughts into words, "I felt like it was a way out. He offered me this new life, where I would have a purpose, get along with my family, and build something from the ground up. I'm not happy studying Forestry, but I have no idea what else to do. This seemed like the perfect solution. And now it's all gone."

"But Miriam," Amber says gently, "are you sure you would have liked working in a restaurant? You have never done that in your life. You don't enjoy working at your parents' store, and those customers leave after a few minutes."

"You haven't met Mrs. Haberstein then," I mutter, referring to one of our chattiest and nosiest customers. She spends on average a good hour in the store, and all of us try to avoid having to serve her. That woman with her incessant gossiping sucks the energy right out of you.

"Well, *most* of them are in and out fairly quickly," Amber amends, smiling. "But at a restaurant, all guests stay as long as your Mrs. Haberstein does. Or longer! Can you really see yourself doing that? Having to serve drunks, listening to people's complaints, while standing there with a smile and apologizing for something you haven't done? Think about it!"

She continues: "Then there's Oliver. You basically don't know him at all, and from what you've told me, you never feel sure of yourself around him. You are nervous and insecure, and you're trying to be someone you think he will like. That's insane! You are such a wonderful person just the way you are, you don't have to change yourself for anyone!" She pauses to take a deep breath, and I look at her meekly.

"Look at me," I whisper, miserably. "I'm fat, I have a weird face, I'm selfish and stupid, and I have no clue what I'm supposed to be doing in life. Who would want me?" Tears start dripping down my face again as I'm saying this.

Amber looks at me, aghast. "Is that how you see yourself?" she asks, stunned. I nod without looking up. It's my dark secret, and I have never told anyone before. I'm convinced that I'm unlovable, that I have nothing to offer to a guy. When I had my two previous boyfriends, I was slim, I did reasonably well in school, and none of us knew what we wanted to do with ourselves afterwards. But now, a couple of years later and twenty-five pounds heavier, I feel left behind. My fellow Forestry-students seem so passionate about their choice, dressing in forest-green clothes already, spending their weekends with hunting buddies out in the woods, and talking about nothing else but soil, ecosystems, and gun calibers. I realized one semester in that I made the wrong choice, but I have no clue what else I should be doing, so I keep plucking along. But I feel like a fraud when I'm sitting in lectures, and the practicum I'll have to do in the fall scares the shit out of me.

And isn't the way my own family treated me proof that I'm unlovable? They put a stranger before their own daughter, because they like him better than me. I'm nothing but a disappointment to them.

Amber, being a sweet and caring friend, tries to convince me otherwise. She tells me that I'm beautiful, that I'm smart and funny and loveable. I nod along to make her feel better, but I know the truth: it's my fault Oliver doesn't want me.

I'm not good enough.

Chapter 5

WHAT DO I WANT?

Life goes on. It's the biggest cliché, yet the biggest truth. Over the next few weeks, I slowly find a semblance of normalcy: attending classes again, working at my part-time job, going out at night. I don't return home, and nobody seems to expect it; I haven't heard from my family in weeks. After it all happened my mother tried to call a few times, but I didn't pick up the phone; she seems to have given up for the moment. *Good.* I know it won't last, but for now I'm ignoring them. It's easier that way. They continue to pay my rent and car insurance, and I continue to live my life as a college student, trying to 'enjoy' being single. I have determined that the best way to get over a man is to get under one, so I'm on the lookout. Not for anything serious, hell no—just a fling to make myself feel better.

There's only one problem: I can't seem to find a guy who wants me.

"You're sending off desperate vibes," a male buddy of mine advises me. "Your entire demeanour basically screams 'love me!' and everywhere you go, you bring your baggage along. Guys can sense that a mile away, that's why they're not biting. Keep your problems at home and pretend you're easy, and you'll get laid in no time, I promise. Guys like nothing more than easy girls."

Hrumph, easier said than done. I have never been good at flirting, and have never had a one-night-stand before. How can you pretend you're easy when you're not? It's beyond me. After being turned down several times, I give up, too humiliated to continue.

Instead of meaningless sex, I develop a strange, antagonistic friendship with Helmut. Helmut is in my class, and he is one of the green-dressed hard-core forest ranger guys, with a full beard (long before it becomes trendy), a hunting lodge he goes to almost every weekend, and a cocky demeanour that irks me. We don't run in the same circles, because he is one of the competitive career-focused guys who take school extremely seriously, and I am not. My focus these days is parties and having fun, and to hang out with people I can have long and drunken conversations about the meaning of life with.

But one night, Helmut bizarrely shows up at a party. This is such an unusual occurrence (and I'm in that slightly hysterical happy mood where you love everyone) that I come up to him and greet him with a hug.

"What are *you* doing here?" I shout into his ear. "Decided to leave your secret lair?"

He seems slightly offended. "What do you mean?" he asks.

"I never see you anywhere but school," I explain. "What do you do for fun?"

Helmut launches into a pompous explanation about the importance of school and "keeping your eyes on the prize," frequently interrupted by me arguing passionately against it.

It's not that I disagree with him on everything, but that fighting with him is so much *fun*. After an hour of heated discussion, we are both thirsty. Helmut offers to get us drinks, and as he walks to the bar, I cock my head and watch him. Could I fall for him? Really embrace the whole Forestry thing? After all, I already started on the path to Forestry, and while I know deep down that it's not for me, what else is? The family business isn't my cup of tea, the restaurant ship has sailed, and I'm fresh out of ideas of what else to do.

I regard him critically as he comes back: the dark, full beard, bad haircut, self-satisfied smile—hmm, he really isn't my type. And he is wearing green again, from head to toe. For the love of God, has he not heard of other colours?

"Do you own any other colours but green?" I challenge him, and we are off again. While I may not find him attractive, and his personality annoys me, I must admit that his confidence and self-assuredness intrigue me. How did he get to be so confident? What's his secret? I decide to find out, and invite him to my place for the next evening.

Deciding what to wear is, as always, difficult. What outfit sends the message that I'm skinny, cute, not interested in a relationship, yet attractive; casual, yet effortlessly put together? If there is an outfit that conveys all that, I don't know what it is. After much consideration, I choose my usual go-to: the only pair of jeans that fit (sort-of) well, and a red-and-white plaid button-down shirt. It hides my tummy, looks casual but not sloppy, and I hope it says, "cute, outdoorsy forest gal with a touch of whimsy."

Helmut, unsurprisingly, wears green again. He told me the night before that he doesn't have many other colours in his closet (ha! I knew it!), which is kind of genius when you think about it: you never have to fret about what to wear. Apparently, he does own a pair of jeans, but he only puts them on for "special occasions." He's a weird guy.

I offer him a drink, and we proceed into my room. Once we've sat down, there's an awkward silence. I desperately search for something to say, to repeat the easy, if combative conversation from last night, but I come up with nothing. Then, Helmut asks me a doozy: "Why did you decide to study Forestry?"

My first impulse is to bristle. How *dare* he question my motive? (I'm questioning it daily, but that's different.) But I resist, and give the question some serious consideration. Why did I choose something so unsuitable for myself?

Should I tell him that I was in *the dark place* for several months when I decided upon it? That my strongest desire was to hide away from people? Nope, I've never told anyone, and I won't start with Helmut.

How about I mention that I find girls stressful, and figured that being in a program where most of my fellow students are male would be easier? Should I also let him in on my deepest secret, my hope to find a hunky, outdoorsy guy as my future husband?

Over my dead body.

My last, *highly* professional criterion is that I love dogs more than I like most people, and the thought of being able to bring my best friend to work every day was so tempting, I thought it would make the rest of the job bearable.

I decide to lead with that.

"I was looking for a job where I can bring my dog to work every day. Dogs make the best co-workers!" I laugh a little, but Helmut stays serious.

"Do you like it?"

I hesitate for a moment. Should I be honest? What the hell, I think to myself. I don't want to impress him, so who cares what he'll think of me.

"Nope," I admit. "I can barely get through the lectures. There's way too much detail about soil and rocks. It's painful. You love it, though, don't you?"

"It's my passion," he agrees. "I've been wanting to become a forest ranger since I was a little boy. My uncle is one, and he's been taking me with him since I was four years old. I love being in the woods. There's nothing else I ever wanted to do."

"That's why you take it so seriously," I realize with sudden understanding. "You don't want to be one of the losers." The first year of our program is notoriously difficult, with 70% of students failing the final exams. I should know, I was one of them last year. This is my second time attending the first two semesters.

"Yup," he agrees. "If this doesn't work out, I don't know what else to do. That's all I ever wanted."

"Must be nice," I say wistfully. "I wish I had your certainty. I have no idea what I want to do with myself."

"Did you really decide on Forestry because of dogs?" Helmut asks me.

"Pretty much," I admit, and we both laugh. "I know it's insane," I allow. "But if you don't know what you want, what are you supposed to do? You have to decide on *something*. I wanted to work for a year before going to school to figure it out, but my parents really pressured me to go to college right away. I know this forest guy who took me along for a week, and thought that there are worse jobs out there. How bad can driving around in your jeep with your dog by your side be? I didn't think school would be so hard." I finish glumly.

"It is," Helmut agrees. "But I think it's harder for you because you're not interested in it. If you really want something, you grit your teeth and fight for it, because you know it will be worth it in the end."

"If you say so," I say. "I wouldn't know. I don't know what I want."

And that's the problem right there: I'm stuck. I know what I don't like (pretty much everything about my life right now)—but what *do* I like? I have absolutely no idea.

Chapter 6

JUST WHEN YOU THINK IT COULDN'T GET ANY WORSE...

Our conversation stays with me. Helmut and I don't hang out one-on-one anymore, but we chat between lectures, and occasionally I join him and the green boys (my nickname for him and his posse) for coffee in the school cafeteria. They mostly ignore me, but I don't care—I think they're weird anyway. I can't quite pinpoint why I sit with them, but I think it's because of the conversation I had with Helmut. For the first time, I have said out loud that I'm doing the wrong thing with my life and now that I have not only admitted it to myself, but also to another person, it's much harder to ignore. Maybe I also hope that some of the green boys' determination to succeed will rub off on me—even though it's been unsuccessful thus far.

Spring has arrived, and with it the busy time at my family's store. It's been two months since I fled my parents' house, and I don't like that we're not talking. I hate tension, and this silence between us has gone on long enough. I'm still hurt, but this situation is getting to me. Lately, I wake up every night, obsessing about it. So, one day I gather all my courage, pick up the phone and call them. My heart is pounding and I'm nervous—how will they react?

"You're alive," my mother greets me. "We hadn't heard from you in so long, we weren't sure."

"The phone works both ways, you know," I counter.

"I tried it three times, you never called me back," she reminds me. Hrumph, touché. I decide to ignore that and move on.

"So, do you need me at the farm market?" I ask. "Spring is here, it's usually busy."

"Yes, we could use another pair of hands," she tells me.

I hesitate for a moment, desperately wanting to know, but also afraid at the same time. "Are Oliver and Emma …?"

"Yes," mom says. "They are together. I'm sorry Miriam, but it looks serious. Oliver started working for us—"

"What?!" I interrupt. "When? *Why?* Doesn't he have the restaurant?"

"He still does, but it's not going well. It's almost always empty, and he's broke. He'll probably have to close. He needs money, and he asked if we needed help. Since he's only open for dinner, he can work during the day. Dad is giving him a chance, and Oliver is really interested in our business! If the restaurant doesn't work out, he may start working full-time for us."

I'm stunned into silence. What the hell? Not only did he take my sister, now he's weaseling his way into the rest of my family as well? I'm getting mad. Doesn't he have a family of his own? Why does he have to steal mine?

"Miriam? Are you still there?" my mother asks.

"Yes, I'm still here. Well, do you even need me when you have precious Oliver?" I challenge petulantly. Big mistake. My mother doesn't handle that kind of whininess well.

"Stop being such a child, Miriam. Of course we want to see you. But you have to learn that the entire world doesn't revolve around you. Oliver is in real trouble, and we can help him. Not only that, have you ever thought about the future of our business? Neither you nor Emma are interested, and that's fine. We never expected you to be. But here's someone who *wants* to learn all about it. It's like a gift from heaven, and you know what? It's really nice to have someone admire us for what we do." She stops to draw breath, and I'm speechless. Speechless, ashamed, and resentful, which is *not* a good mix. I want her to feel guilty and wanting to make it up to me, and instead she turns it around and makes *me* feel like the ungrateful one. This phone call hasn't gone at all as I expected. Instead of feeling better, I'm now feeling worse. I want to simultaneously hit something and hide under the covers. I tell my mother that I'll come on the weekend, and hang up.

I have to digest this new development. It's a nightmare! The guy I never want to see again in my life is not only dating my sister, but he's also working for the family now? Which means that every time I come home, he'll be around? I can't believe it. It couldn't possibly get any worse.

Oh, but it can.

As I come home three days later, I learn something that my mother didn't get around to telling me since I hung up rather quickly: my parents decided to renovate the empty space above the store and rent it out. Can you guess to whom?

I bet you can: Oliver.

"You're not serious." I stare at them both, appalled. "He's going to live across the street from us? For real? I will have to see him—with Emma— every single time I come home?"

"Miriam, try to see it from our perspective. And Oliver's. When he cancels the lease on his restaurant, he will have to move out of his apartment as well. We have an empty apartment, and he offered to renovate it—it makes sense."

"But, but," I stammer, desperately trying to make them understand how atrocious this situation is. "Don't you get how awkward and weird that is for me? He dumped me, and instead of trying to forget him and everything that happened, he's right under my nose, banging my sister, working with you, and living right across the damn street!" I'm yelling the last bit, I'm so enraged. *How can they not get it?*

"Your life isn't here, it's in Munich," my mother counters, voice raised as well. "You'll probably not come back once you're done with school. You will live your own life, somewhere else. And then we will have made a sacrifice for no reason, because you will be gone anyway, and we still won't have anybody who's interested in working alongside us. Is that what you want?"

She looks at me sternly. I don't know what to say. Deep down I get the sense that there is some truth in her words, but I'm unwilling to be reasonable right now. I'm too worked up and mad.

"Just don't expect me to be nice to him," are my final words, and then I leave.

I grab my jacket and Roxy and half run, half power-walk away from the house. I need to be away from them, to clear my head and figure out what I should do.

The way I see it, there are two options:

A) Leave and never come back. It's tempting right at this moment, but I know I could never pull it off. I'm not tough enough to keep it up for longer than a few weeks. I cracked last time, didn't I? Also, where would I go for summer break and Christmas?

B) Try to rise above it and be the bigger person. Ugh, that's going to be hard. But the longer I walk and think about it, the more I come to the conclusion that this is my only choice. I don't have to forgive him (never!), but I can act cool and pretend I don't care about him at all. Let him think I got over our little romance in no time!

The next day is my first opportunity to test my resolve. I haven't seen him since that fateful day in our kitchen, when I realized that he and my sister were an item.

On the way to work my stomach clenches painfully from nerves and my hands are damp. I wish I could turn around and run away, but I firmly tell myself that I am strong, and that I got this!

When I get to our stall at the market square, I furtively glance around to see if he's already here.

He is. As soon as I lay eyes on him, I'm hit by a wave of anguish and longing so strong, my knees buckle underneath me and I have to lean against a wall.

Shit. *Shit, shit, shit.* I forgot how tall he is. How handsome. I can't do this, it's too painful. They can't expect me to work with him like nothing happened. I take some deep, slow breaths, trying to get my wildly beating heart to slow down. After a few minutes, it finally does, and I get up. I can't stay here forever, crouched against the wall. "You *can* do this," I tell myself again. "He's just a guy. Ignore him. Pretend he doesn't exist."

On shaking legs, I head over to my dad and the rest of the staff. They are unloading the truck and filling up our market stand with fresh fruit and produce. I grab a box of lettuce, carry it over, and start piling the heads of lettuce on top of each other. Out of the corner of my eye, I see Oliver on the far end of the stand, stacking empty crates. He doesn't look up, but he is bright red in the face. Being a redhead, he blushes furiously whenever he is embarrassed or flustered, and right now his face is as red as a fire engine. So, he feels awkward too. *Good.* Somehow, seeing him discombobulated makes me feel calmer. There won't be any open confrontation, of that I'm sure now.

And there isn't. The first customers arrive soon, bringing with them the distraction we desperately need. We manage to get through the morning without talking to each other at all. I even joke around with Pete, my favourite co-worker, who has worked for us for nearly 30 years, first for my grandfather, now my father. On the outside he appears gruff, but he has a heart of gold. He also has a dry sense of humour, and the two of us always have fun together.

By the end of the workday, I feel proud of myself. I got through it without breaking down! (The first five minutes don't count.) There was one sticky moment where I literally bumped into Oliver, because my head was turned towards a customer while I was walking away. The moment our bodies collided an electric charge went through me, and I stared up at him, open-mouthed and slightly breathless. He looked back at me, an unreadable expression on his face. I mumbled, "Oops, sorry," and moved away quickly. I'm dazed as I replay what just happened: my first words to him after his betrayal, and *I'm* apologizing to *him*. I'm so annoyed about that, that I refuse to think about how it felt when his body touched mine and concentrate on my irritation instead. It helps.

This becomes our new pattern: I come home again on weekends to work, and Oliver and I largely ignore each other. Emma is at her job on Saturdays, so I don't see her at the market. I know that she has moved into his apartment above the restaurant, but I try to think as little as possible about it. We currently don't talk.

My mother and I have found an uneasy truce, maintaining it by not talking about anything personal. It's small talk only, largely town gossip and some highly-censored tidbits about school. Exams are coming up, and studying for them keeps me so busy that I manage to forget for hours at a time how messed up my life is.

Never at night, though. At night, my demons come out to play. I have trouble sleeping and lay awake for hours, tears silently rolling down my cheeks, soaking my pillow. I have this one, big question running through my mind on repeat: what am I going to do? *What am I going to do?*

I can't see myself ever being happy again. Even though I have friends,

I feel utterly alone. I try to act like I'm fine, and I think I'm doing a pretty good job going through the motions: I laugh at jokes, I study with my study group, I work. But inside, I feel dead. Whenever I'm out with people, I can't wait to get away from them to be alone. But when I'm by myself, I can't stand being alone with my thoughts, and make sure that I have enough background noise to drown out my negative inner voice. The radio, TV, and audiobooks become absolute necessities to my survival. I'm terrified of what might happen when my inner voice gets a chance to list everything that's wrong with me.

And then, the semester is done. The exams are finished, the parties are over, and everybody is packing up to leave for the long summer break. In the fall, we will start our practicum, which involves working in the forest for five months. I got a placement close to home, which at the time seemed like a lucky break—free rent and meals! Now I'm dreading it. Amber and I decided to cancel the lease on our apartment to save money, which means I have no place to go but home. Eight months stretch interminably in front of me, and I wonder how I will survive them.

Well, at least I won't be bored. I'm still unpacking boxes in my old bedroom when my parents both come in, closing the door behind them. Uh-oh, they want to talk. I brace myself for the conversation, having the distinct feeling that it won't be good news.

"We want to ask you something," my mother begins.

"Okay," I say cautiously. "What is it?"

"What are your plans for summer break?" she asks.

"Nothing much," I admit. They already know that a friend and I want to go camping for a week, but apart from that, I have no idea what to do during my ten weeks off.

"Well, we thought if you have nothing else going on, you could help renovate the apartment. There's still lots to do, and none of us has the time." She hasn't mentioned whose apartment—she doesn't need to. I *know*. But I still want her to spell it out.

"Help whom?" I ask innocently.

"You know whom I'm talking about," she says impatiently. "Oliver."

I'm not even surprised. In their minds, it makes perfect sense. My parents work six days a week, my sister has a full-time job, and I'm the only one with the luxury of too much free time on her hands. My parents never tire of reminding me that we have a family business, and that everybody has to help. They also believe that Oliver and I have been working together without a problem for months. Either they choose to ignore the fact that we don't talk to each other, or they really haven't noticed.

Do I have a choice? Not really. I can't sit around the house all summer while everybody else is working their asses off. So, I shrug my shoulders and mutter, "I guess so."

"That's great," she says. My father opens his mouth for the first time since entering my bedroom, and says quietly, "Thank you, Miriam."

Hearing him say that makes me feel marginally better.

The next morning, I reluctantly walk up the stairs to the first-floor apartment. We used to rent it out to a family of four, but they moved out a couple of years ago, and we haven't done anything with the space since. Surveying it now, I see that it's pretty run-down. The wallpaper is peeling, the carpets are stained and give off a bad smell, and the kitchen is a write-off: the stove doesn't work, most of the cabinet doors are broken or off their hinges, and opening the fridge door is a mistake. The stench that hits me is so powerful, I feel like I got slapped in the face.

"Yuck, gross!" I yell out involuntarily, and slam the door shut as fast as I can. It doesn't look like they have been doing much here at all—I thought Oliver had been working on this place?

It becomes evident what he has been up to when I walk out of the kitchen into the living/dining room. Where there used to be a solid ceiling, there is now an opening to the attic above, with a spiral staircase leading up to it. I climb up the staircase into the attic, and my breath catches in my throat; this space has the potential to be *amazing*. It's a big, airy room with slanted ceilings and enough windows to be bright and flooded with light. The wood floor is in surprisingly good condition, and probably doesn't need much work apart from sanding and staining.

I feel a big lump forming in my throat as I slowly walk through the space, picturing what it may look like once it's done. Visions of cozy nights curled up on the sofa come unbidden in my mind. Right there, under the window, would be a perfect spot for a big, comfy armchair, where one could sit with a book and a glass of wine, reading for hours. Or you could make it into a bedroom, with the bed placed below the skylight, so you could see the stars at night.

It's not for you, my inner voice reminds me harshly. *Stop making plans.* She's right. I must quit this immediately, or I'm going to break down. As I turn around, I jump in fright. Oliver stands there, watching me. I didn't hear him come up, too caught up in my own thoughts.

"Fuck, you scared me!" I yelp, clutching my hand to my heart. Who am I, a tragic movie heroine from the last century? Well, not with the swearing, I remind myself wryly, and that thought makes me smile for a moment.

"Sorry," he says softly. The way he looks at me, I get the sense that he's apologizing for much more than startling me. Is he going to explain why he dumped me? Why he chose my sister over me? Will I hear a real apology? Or is he going to inform me of everything that's wrong with me, and tell me uncomfortable truths I'd rather not hear? I stand there motionless, immobilized by sudden fear and hope. Maybe this is it, I can't help but wish for. An explanation, *finally.*

But before he can say anything, a loud voice from below interrupts us.

"Hey, is anybody here? Helloooo?!?"

"That must be Eddie," Oliver says, and calls out, "we're up here!" A wave of disappointment mixed with relief washes over me. The moment for revelations is over.

A man clomps up the stairs, breathing heavily and guzzling a can of Red Bull. He is tall, with long, unkempt dark hair, a big belly, and a loud, booming voice. Eddie is the general contractor, and he takes Oliver aside to talk about numerous problems that have cropped up—typical renovation stuff. Before they have their little man chat, I'm being sent away like a naughty school girl, having been given the task of removing the wallpaper in one of the bedrooms downstairs.

Fuming, I start ripping wallpaper off the wall. It's a great way to relieve aggression, and I take full advantage of it by attacking the walls with a vengeance.

While I'm doing it, I reflect on the parody that my life has become. Here I am, working on my ex-lover's and sister's love nest. How fucked up is that? And why am I doing it? Have I become such a spineless push-over that I meekly do whatever other people tell me to do? It appears that way. But I can change. I *have* to change, if I want to regain at least an ounce of self-respect. I'm ripping and plotting all day, and at the end of it, I have a plan. Well, at least sort of. The objective of my plan is simple: getting away. That night, I take my address book and a calendar, and start making phone calls. I talk to every friend who ever mentioned getting together during summer break, and don't hang up until we have made firm plans. My two best friends from school have come through for me, with Amber offering me to visit her at her mother's place in Weilheim, and Todd inviting me to come to Berlin with him to visit his friend Micah. These two invites combined with the camping trip I have planned for next month mean that I have half of summer break taken care of.

I decide to worry about the rest later, and go tell my parents that I suddenly have plans for the summer and won't be staying. They take it surprisingly well, given how they stress the importance of work over play. But I suspect that they do feel guilty about everything that went down, and even if they didn't—I'm a grown woman of twenty-one, and they can't make me stay here. I have been working part-time jobs ever since I was twelve years old, so I have a nice little nest egg in my bank account, enough money to last me throughout the summer.

I pack my bags, spend one last, sleepless night in my childhood bedroom, and then I *run*.

That summer is a blur. Todd and I stay a week at his friend's Micah's place in Berlin, and I fall in love with the city. I borrow Micah's bike, and spend hours every day pedaling through the city, soaking it all in. In the afternoons, we meet up again, either getting drunk or stoned, and philosophising about life. After two days, Micah and I hook up, and I have the fling I so desperately wanted. To my dismay, it doesn't make me feel better—it's all wrong. I don't want to sound awful, but—he's a small guy. Shorter than me, and weighs probably twenty pounds less than I do. Everything on his body is in proportion, which means, when we're having sex for the first time, I'm not sure if he's entered me yet or not. I actually ask in a whisper, "Are you in?" feeling terrible when he answers in the affirmative. But—I can't feel him! Maybe we could have figured it out over time, but after that one time, we don't sleep together again.

Instead, Micah and I cuddle and talk deep into the night, and that part is nice.

However, when we say goodbye after the week I know I won't be seeing him again, and I feel mostly relieved about it.

After Berlin, Weilheim is a stark contrast. Amber's mother lives on a little farm in the south of Germany, raising chickens, geese, and sheep. She also has a dog and four cats, who drape themselves all over the furniture. I love animals, so I'm thrilled. It's all so pretty! The house is a gorgeously remodeled old farmhouse, situated in a little meadow surrounded by forest on three sides. The next neighbour is on the other side of the valley, so far away that I can just make out the house in the distance, as small as a child's toy. Amber's mother is a passionate gardener, and has created an enchanted garden. It is beautiful, quiet and peaceful—*too* peaceful.

The silence is getting to me. The nights are so quiet that I can't sleep. The voice in my head is deafening, and I can't escape it. It is taunting me, telling me what a screw-up I am.

"Look at you, trying to run away from your problems. Don't you know that you can't escape them? Don't you realize that your problem is *you*?"

It's awful. The only thing I can do to escape the voice for a while is reading, and luckily, I brought my best friend along: Harry Potter. Getting lost in his magical world always makes me feel better.

The sleepless nights and restlessness I can't hide cause friction between Amber and me. She is getting annoyed by my bad mood, my inability to enjoy the little paradise her mother has created here. I feel terrible about it, but can't seem to get out of my funk. To avoid a full-blown fight, I get into the habit to go for long walks in the woods, taking Harry Potter with me, to hide from everybody. The weather is beautiful, and I try to be grateful for this escape from my normal life, but I fail miserably. The long hours give me too much time to think, and there are not enough distractions.

But even the longest week comes to an end eventually. On the day of our departure I thank Amber's mother profusely for having me, trying to hide how eager I am to get going. As beautiful as her place is, it's way too quiet for someone who doesn't want introspection. What I'm craving is noise and distraction, not peace and quiet.

I'm getting just that at my friend Sarah's place. Her parents are old hippies, and their house is pleasantly ramshackle and chaotic. I *love* it. There are always people coming and going, friends of her two younger brothers, neighbours, Sarah's boyfriend. Everybody is always welcome, because Sarah's parents seem to genuinely love people. For someone like me, who grew up in a household that was the opposite, this is fantastic. Overwhelming, for sure, but exactly what I need right now. Sarah takes me horseback riding, and we hang out all day at the barn, cleaning the stalls, grooming the horses, and chatting to the other people there. I find the horses incredibly soothing, and spend a lot of time pressing myself close against their warm sides.

Sarah and I go swimming, to the movies, to the pub. She is an easy-going person, and she acts like one of the guys; we only talk about inconsequential, easy stuff. No more delving into messy feelings for the time being; I'm talked out.

Sarah seems to sense that. Or maybe she simply isn't interested in my messy life, and that's fine by me.

Chapter 7
"HE STARTED DRIPPING"

In September, my practicum starts. The Forestry program consists of six theoretical semesters and two practical ones. In this first practicum, I am to work mostly with the lumberjacks, learning how to plant, how a harvester works, and yes, how to cut down trees with a chainsaw. For that purpose, we start the practicum by going on a week-long chainsaw-course where I'm reunited with some of my classmates. We have classes all day, and party all night. The atmosphere is festive, and has a definite summer camp flair about it. I'm enjoying myself much more than expected, and by the end of the week I have successfully managed to chop down a tree all by myself.

After that, I'm to meet the forest ranger for the first time. I agonize about what to wear, regretting my refusal to buy proper green forest pants. Are jeans appropriate?

I have good reason to worry about the dress code: I've gotten work-wear spectacularly wrong in pretty much every job I've ever had.

When I did my one-week orientation the previous year, I showed up in short hiking shorts, rugged hiking boots, and a Fjällräven button-down tucked into the shorts. (In the likely event that you have no idea what the funnily spelled 'Fjällräven' is, let me enlighten you: it's a Swedish brand that makes outdoorsy clothes and backpacks. Their logo is a cute fox, rolled together like he's asleep. It's stitched in red yarn on my white-and-blue checkered shirt. So adorable!)

I paid a hundred dollars for the shirt, and I was sure I looked very woodsy.

I didn't.

The manager took one look at me, raised his eyebrows, and told me, "You shouldn't wear shorts to work." I blushed magenta and wanted to sink into the ground. Is there a more horrible feeling than getting an outfit completely wrong?

Well yes, there is, but in that moment, I couldn't have been more embarrassed. I apologized profusely, and felt extremely uncomfortable for the rest of the day.

Several years later, I did it again. I showed up for my first day at a new job (a farmer's market—more about that later) in inappropriate clothes, i.e. a top that was too low-cut for my boss' liking. I have small breasts, and it wasn't *that* low, so it didn't look obscene—but I later found out that the entire management was extremely religious, and any amount of cleavage was too much cleavage. Again, there was much blushing, apologizing, and feeling uncomfortable all day.

We're not done yet. Fast forward another couple of years, and I'm doing another orientation, this time at a hospital (it will be the hospital I spend six years working at, but I don't know that yet) as pre-requisite for the college I desperately want to get into. *This time,* I have sworn to myself that I will get it right. This is too important! I decide to 'suit up.' Barney Stinson swears by suits, and what's good enough for Barney will help me make a great first impression—right?

Wrong. I didn't take into consideration that the trousers are too long (I should have gotten them hemmed, but haven't), and to avoid them dragging along the floor (nothing looks more unprofessional), I have to wear heels.

I check my appearance before leaving, taking in the white shirt (slightly yellowed under the armpits, but if I keep the jacket on, nobody will notice), slightly ill-fitting grey suit, and the pointy-toed heels. There's no cleavage or excess skin anywhere. Will that do?

When I show up in the Medical Imaging Department, the first thing I notice are the employees' shoes: universally practical and comfortable. It's runners, clogs, and granny-shoes as far as the eye can see! Uh-oh. The lady who meets me greets me friendly enough, but then she adds, "Are you going to be okay on your feet all day, with your heels?"

Duh. I lie and say that I will be, "Fine, just fine!" laughing nervously and dying a bit inside.

Do you notice a theme here? Wedding, jobs, important first impressions (including meeting the love of my life—stay tuned for chapter 11!) all involve poor clothing choices on my part. Despite loving clothes so much! It's not fair. No wonder I could never hack it as a fashion blogger.

Anyway, where was I?

Oh yes, the difficult question of what to wear. In the end I choose jeans, hiking boots, a thick sweater, and my prized possession: a North Face rain jacket, in green! My only green piece of clothing. To my relief, my outfit doesn't elicit any comment or raised eyebrows, so I figure I must have done all right.

The forest ranger is heavy-set, with a large, crooked nose, thick hair cut short in a buzzcut, and a goofy sense of humour. His name is Conrad, and we meet at his office that's located in the basement of his house. The first week is easy: we mostly drive around, do some office work, and talk about the job and after a few days, about a whole bunch of other stuff as well. It's very relaxed, which makes me feel even more apprehensive about week two: working side-by-side with the lumberjacks. I'm nervous. What if they don't want to work with a girl? What if it's too hard, and I can't make it through the day? And, always my biggest fear: what if they don't like me?

I've met them before, on my rounds with Conrad. But that was different; the boss was there, and they didn't say much. Now, on my first day alone with them, we introduce ourselves properly.

Butch is the younger one of the two, probably in his mid-thirties. He is tall and slender, with dark hair and stubble on his face, and always a cigarette in the corner of his mouth. Gus is at least fifteen years older, short and compact, with a neatly shaved face and a friendly smile. He's the more talkative of the two, and takes me under his wing.

On our first day, we are planting beech seedlings as part of the effort to reshape the forest into the more natural way it used to be, before humans planted everything with the fast-growing, high profit-yielding spruce. While it's by far an easier job than cutting down trees, my back starts to hurt after a couple of hours, my knees are sore from kneeling down, and a slight drizzle has started to fall. It's only mid-September, but here in the Fichtelgebirge mountains, temperatures are hovering at only five degrees Celsius, and a cold wind makes me shiver.

But I don't know Butch and Gus. While they work steadily, they also take regular, leisurely breaks. After all, who's going to tell on them? There's no time clock to punch in and out of, and when the boss stops by they can always pretend they just started their break. As the drizzle gets stronger, they pack their things and announce it's break time. We hop into Butch's beat-up car, and he drives us to a construction trailer about ten minutes away. As I step in, warmth envelopes me like a welcoming hug. "It's so warm in here!" I cry out in happy surprise, and both men laugh.

"Of course it is," Butch says, grinning widely. "Gus gets a fire started in the stove," he points to a black potbelly stove in the corner, "every morning before we start. Has been doing that for thirty years."

I turn to Gus, with a huge smile on my face. "Gus, I love you."

The boys seem pleased to have a fresh face in their tired old two-some, and get more and more talkative as the days pass. Gus tells me that they have found several suicide victims in the woods over the years. "One of them had hung himself so high up in the trees, we would have never seen him," he tells me conversationally over lunch one day. "But he started dripping, and that's how we found him." I choke on my sandwich, and Gus pats my back until I can breathe again.

"What?" I splutter, stunned. "People come into the woods to kill themselves?"

"Oh yes," Gus says calmly. "Lots of them do. Mostly hangings. A few shoot themselves. And one guy connected a hose to the exhaust pipe of his car and died of carbon monoxide poisoning."

I just stare at him, stunned into silence. Suicide is something that scares the hell out of me. I've had a shitty time over the last little while, but I never considered suicide, not even for a minute. How desperate were these people to see no way out? To have given up so completely, they decided to erase their future?

"How was it?" I ask, in morbid fascination. "To find a dead person?"

Gus shrugs. "It is what it is," he says matter-of-factly. "I feel sorry for the poor buggers. I knew one of them. He lived close to me, I knew him and his wife. Rumour has it she had an affair, and I guess it ended up being true, seeing what he did to himself. Stupid bastard, should have gotten rid of the wife instead of himself."

He means he should have *divorced* her. Not killed her.

I think.

Only a few weeks in, I quickly realize two things:

1. I love working with the guys. They are simple men, but honest and funny. They also have a streak of old-fashioned gentlemanliness in them, never letting me carry anything too heavy, making sure I am warm enough, watching out if I can keep up. Like I said, I *love* them.

2. I'm absolutely, completely, 100% in the wrong line of work. I thought I would enjoy being out in the woods, but to my dismay, I don't. It's cold, dark, and monotonous. There's barely any variety, just one spruce tree after another. But the worst of it is that I *hate* the work. Turns out, physical labour is not my thing. It sounds good in theory: getting fit while doing worthwhile work that protects the earth? Yes, please! But the reality is that it is tedious and boring, while simultaneously being cold and strenuous. It's a terrible combination.

However, there is a way out. Conrad and I get on like a house on fire. We talk easily about a wide variety of topics, from forestry-related stuff to the meaning of life. I have noticed that if we have a good conversation going, he will keep me with him that day, instead of having me work with the guys. In a desperate attempt at self-preservation, I take advantage of that.

We develop a friendship. At first, it's harmless and solely restricted to work. But slowly, it becomes more intense. It doesn't have a sexual component, but it is deeply intimate. I start telling him about the Oliver situation, about my many insecurities, and how lost I am. He tells me about his problems, worries, and passions. He is an outdoorsy guy, and loves to go skiing, hiking, and paragliding. One day he offers me to come along with his family to a day of skiing. I only hesitate for a moment—what else do I have going on?—before saying yes.

I have already met his wife and ten-year old son, since his office is in his home, and we usually meet there in the mornings before work. I feel awkward at first, intruding on their family outing, but the awkwardness fades as the pleasure of the activity takes over. I haven't gone skiing in several years, and I forgot how much fun it is. Zipping down the hill, with the wind whipping around my face and the thrill (mixed with a bit of fear) of the speed makes me forget all my problems. I love it, and at the end of the day, thank them all profusely for taking me along.

"No problem," Conrad says. "Let's do it again, ok?"

And we do. From that day on, I tag along regularly. Not only do we go skiing in the mountains close to us, they also go for weekend trips to Austria and take me with them. I go, because I'll take any opportunity to escape my house, but I try not to think too much about this weird arrangement we have. I like to pretend that I'm like a daughter to them, but I know that's not true.

Conrad likes my company. Does he like me? I know he does, but I don't want to know how much. His wife plays along, for reasons I can't fathom. Their son is thrilled to have someone to play with, and makes this whole, weird situation feel a bit more normal.

And me? Why am I tagging along?

Because I'm so lonely. Being back at home, away from my friends, is incredibly hard. I still avoid my sister, only saying the bare minimum to her. My parents have each other, and our relationship is still strained as well. All I do, apart from working, is hide in my room, read, and drown my feelings in candy, carbs and chocolate.

Chapter 8
THE BEGINNING OF AN IDEA

The text comes on one of those bleak evenings. I have eaten so many sour candies that my tongue has started to bleed, and I feel sick to my stomach and sick of myself.

It reads: *"Hi Miriam, how's it going? I'm organizing a weekend at a cabin in my forest district. It's rustic, but pretty. You in?"*

The text is from Toby, a guy from my class I started hanging out with only weeks before the end of the last semester. He is tall, handsome, and we have no romantic interest in each other whatsoever. He's one of those guys who is friends with lots of girls, because he's simply a nice, easy-going guy. It's great, because I love talking to him. Toby is a passionate traveller, and has backpacked through Africa, Europe, and parts of Asia. I'm fascinated by his stories, and wish I would have the courage to just up and leave. A weekend away is just what the doctor ordered, and I enthusiastically say yes.

A couple of weeks later, we all arrive in the Black Forest. There are eight of us: four guys and four girls. The cabin is indeed rustic, with one big kitchen with a wood stove, a small bathroom (hurray! I wasn't sure if there would be one), and two bedrooms with two bunk beds in each. It's all dark wood, and the mounted deer heads on the walls confirm that the cabin is mostly used by hunters. Hunting is part of our education, but we haven't gotten that far yet; none of us has a hunting license. The objective for the weekend is different: we want to eat, drink, and have fun.

And that's just what we do. On the first night, we all cook chili together, and after dinner we decide to go on a night walk. It's the end of January, bitterly cold, but we heat up a huge pot of mulled wine, fill several thermos flasks, and bundle up. The night is clear, with the snow being lit up by the moon and stars, illuminating the forest with a shimmering, silvery light.

Soon, we form groups of twos and threes. I'm walking with Toby and Sandra, who brought her dog Walter with her. Walter is a Dachshund, and we watch him as his short legs struggle with the deep snow. He has to hop to get through, which makes him look like a sausage-shaped rabbit, but he doesn't seem to mind. On the contrary, he has a big goofy smile on his face, and his skinny tail is wagging the entire time.

"Your dog knows how to enjoy life," I comment, smiling down at Walter.

"Yup, he sure does," Sandra confirms. "He's never had a bad day in his life."

"Wouldn't that be nice," I muse.

"You know, it's actually pretty easy," Sandra says. "I've learnt a lot from Walter over the years, and you know what?" She pauses, looking at us with a glint in her eyes and a mischievous smile.

"What?" we both ask in unison.

Sandra pauses a moment longer to heighten the suspense, and then proclaims with a flourish, "I have figured out the secret to happiness."

"Oh, yeah?" Toby challenges. "If that's true, you can quit school right now, because once you sell your secret, you will be filthy rich. Everybody wants to know the secret to happiness."

While they joke around, my gaze drifts upwards towards the starry sky. The secret to happiness—I would give an arm and a leg to discover what it is. I can't figure out how to be happy. Is the solution to my problem right here, walking next to me? Could it be *that* easy?

"So, what is it?" I eventually ask, interrupting Toby and Sandra's banter.

Sandra looks at me, and something in my face must tell her that I'm not in the mood for any more jokes. So, she takes a deep breath, and then shares Walter's philosophy:

"First, you have to live in the moment. Walter loves every moment of every day. If we are in lecture, he's happy to roll up in a ball by my feet and take a snooze. If we go for a drive, he's happy to go along, and he doesn't care for how long he'll be in the car. If we are out, he's delirious with happiness about being out, no matter the weather." We all inadvertently look at him frolicking in the snow, having the time of his life, despite his short legs.

"Second, don't hold grudges. I may be gone all day, but when I come home, he's happiness personified. I think he minds when I leave, but the moment I'm back, it's all forgotten. All he cares about is that I'm back now, and he's grateful for that."

Our family dog Roxy is the same, and I have always envied her ability to enjoy our presence without begrudging our absences. I know this is a much better way to live life, but how do you get there? Can someone retrain my brain, please?

"Third, and I think that's the most important one: accept yourself for who you are. I mean, just look at him"—once again, all three of us turn to look at Walter, who is currently rolling in the snow, his tongue lolling off to the side comically—"could he *be* any more at peace with himself? He has so much going against him: his short legs, weirdly long body, always being the shortest amongst all the dogs. But do you think he gives a shit? I can tell you, he doesn't. He struts his stuff like he's hot as hell, and seems to think the world of himself. And you know what? He should. He makes me happier than most people I have met in my life, and I love everything about him, even his smelly farts."

Finished, Sandra plops herself down on a bench that's conveniently located next to the path we've been walking on. The rest of the gang has disappeared, and it's just the three of us and Walter. Toby and I sit down on each side of Sandra, and none of us says anything for a moment.

Eventually, Toby states drily, "Sandy, you're a fucking genius."

I couldn't agree more.

For the rest of the weekend, I keep thinking about "Walter's three steps to happiness," as I call them. I have been doing the opposite to all of them: instead of living in the moment, I keep obsessing about the past and worrying about the future. I have a huge, mega-grudge against my family and Oliver, and it's not helping me one bit. Instead of moving on, I'm stuck in an endless loop of resentment and self-pity. And I don't like myself. I'm disgusted by the weight I've piled on, I despise my smoking, and I feel like a loser. I don't know if I'm a nice person or not, I don't know if I'm a smart person or not—I don't know anything about myself. I base my likeability on other people—if people like me, I must be likeable, right? But it's a stressful way to live. I'm constantly worried about what other people think of me, and if I get the feeling someone doesn't care for me, it plunges me into an existential crisis.

However, this weekend is reviving me and giving me new hope. I'm so energized by the camaraderie and our talks, that I make three resolutions:

1. To quit smoking.

2. To travel this summer.

3. To learn to like myself.

On the last night, I sidle up to Toby to get started on resolution number two. I have never travelled by myself, and I don't know where to begin. That's my first question to him.

"How do you travel alone?"

He turns to me, eyes sparkling with enthusiasm. Toby *loves* to talk travel. "Why do you ask? Have you finally decided to become a world traveller, young grasshopper?" I laugh and shake my head.

"Not a world traveller quite yet," I say, "but I've always wanted to see Canada. I figure, if I don't do it now, I'll never do it. But I'm terrified! And I don't know what to do! Do you just book a ticket and go?"

"Well, you could," Toby starts, settling more comfortably into the old couch we're both sitting on. "I've done that a few times. A few years ago, I packed my backpack, went to the airport, and looked at flights leaving that day. I didn't know where I wanted to go, so I let fate make that decision for me. I flew to Rome that day, and then spent three weeks backpacking through Italy. It was great fun!"

I look at him wide-eyed. "Let's ignore the fact that I would *never* be able to do that. Where do you go from the airport?"

"To a youth hostel," Toby explains. "They are everywhere, they are cheap, and you will find people there who are doing the same thing you do. You can ask for recommendations, or join someone so you can travel together for a while. Seriously, you won't be alone for long, unless you want to be."

"What about the language?" I ask. "Does everybody speak English?" My own English is poor, another reason why I think I should travel. I want to improve it, but I'm also afraid that I don't speak it well enough to get by.

"Yes, most people do, at least a little bit. You will find quite a few Germans on the road, we are committed travellers. But it's honestly not a big deal. Bring a dictionary along, use your hands and feet, and you will be fine."

I'm quiet for a moment, absorbing it all. The thought of going for it, to fly to Canada by myself, is in equal parts tantalizing and terrifying. I have never even been on a plane before! Never gone anywhere by myself! Do I dare?

Toby seems to read my mind, because he continues, "You don't have to backpack by yourself if you don't want to. You could ask Andrea if she wants to go with you—I know she's thinking of going to the west coast of Canada this summer as well." Andrea is one of our fellow students, and to be honest, I find her a bit weird.

"Maybe I will," I say vaguely. "But if that doesn't work out, what other options are there?"

"You could do a work and travel program," Toby suggests.

"What's that?"

"It's a Visa that allows you to work abroad. If you're worried about not knowing where to go at first, you could organize a place from here, so you have a home base to start from."

"That sounds good," I say with mounting excitement. "What kind of work?"

"Oh, all sorts. Often, it's farms and ranches that are looking for help, so I imagine you would feed and clean the animals, maybe help with the harvest. I have never done it, but a friend of mine has, and she really liked it."

"Oh, my God, can you imagine how awesome that would be?" I say. "Working with horses during the day, sitting around a campfire at night, listening to stories about bears and wolves and the wilderness…" I trail off, picturing myself sitting next to a handsome cowboy, his arm around me, promising me a new life in Canada…

"I *have* to go," I say determinedly.

"To Canada!" Toby calls, and raises his beer.

"To Canada," I reply, and we clink bottles.

"Cheers!"

After that weekend, I'm more cheerful than I have been in months. Having a plan, even if it's a crazy one that seems unattainable, has given me a purpose and an energy I haven't felt for a long time. I may not have figured out my entire future yet, but I know where I want to be in six months: in Canada.

I have also kept my resolution to quit smoking, and haven't had a single cigarette since the weekend in the Black Forest. I smoked for about four years, mostly socially, because everybody else did it. Only over the last year have I started to buy cigarettes regularly, but never really enjoyed it. Quitting is a relief, and I never smoke again.

Chapter 9
GOING FOR IT (DESPITE MYSELF)

My practicum comes to an end, and the new semester starts. I move into a tiny apartment on the third floor of a student dormitory that I share with one other person. The bathroom looks like one of those minuscule motorhome bathrooms, where the floor, walls, and ceiling are made of plastic, and the entire room gets wet when you have a shower. It's windowless and so small, when you sit on the toilet you can easily reach all four walls around you.

The galley-style kitchen consists of a two-burner stove, a sink, a small fridge, and a row of hanging cabinets on one side. On the other side is a table that seats two (not very big) people. The window above it is set high in the wall and it is round, giving the kitchen a nautical look.

My bedroom is a pleasant surprise: it is large and sunny, and it comes furnished with a single bed, a wardrobe, and a desk and chair. The windows are facing a green field and some trees, and in the distance, I can see airplanes rising into the sky from the nearby airport. They are a welcome reminder that soon, I will be on board of one of them.

On move-in day, I curse the lack of an elevator and my stubborn refusal to ask anyone for help. I have to haul all my belongings up three flights of stairs, which takes me all morning. When I'm finally done, I collapse onto my bed, sweating and out of breath. However, I can't help but grin widely as I look around me. I *love* this place. Despite the horrible bathroom and the teeny tiny kitchen, this apartment feels like home. For the first time in eight months, I have my own place again.

Later that day I meet my roommate for the first time. Her name is Helen, and she is a spitfire. She has red curly hair, a curvy yet slender body I envy immediately, and a mouth that never shuts up. At twenty-one, she's already divorced, and within an hour I know most of her life story. She's a bit crazy, but easy-going and, even more important in a roommate, she is *clean*. She studies landscape design, and since we're both working, and Helen is dating energetically, we don't see each other very often.

Across from my student dormitory is the computer lab. I don't have my own computer, so I go there to check my emails and to hesitantly figure out how to work a computer. Despite being twenty-two years old and a college student, I have thus far managed to avoid using them. I only sent my first email less than a year ago, a fact that is both embarrassing and astonishing. But now, with my goal of wanting to travel in the summer, I figure I should learn how to use the Internet.

On a cold, blustery March afternoon, I sit down in front of my favourite computer in the back corner by the window. After checking my emails (there are barely any, since I don't send any emails out), I click around on my college's website. There is a community board that people use to list things to sell or buy, when looking for carpooling, and other miscellaneous stuff. I idly scroll through it, when suddenly, I come across this ad:

"Who is interested in doing a practicum in Canada? We live in Canada's Wild West and are looking for students who would like to help at the ranch. Many great outdoor activities available. For more information, contact […]"

An electric shock goes through me, and the hair at the back of my neck stands up. This is *exactly* what I have been looking for! The ad is in German, which may be because it's posted on a German website. But I fervently hope that the lady speaks at least a little bit of German. I'm so excited, I run home, grab my German-English dictionary, and run back to the lab to write a reply. It is short, but it takes me the better part of an hour, because I'm not used to writing in English.

The result looks like this:

"Hi Rose! I found your advertisement on my school's website, and I am very interested to learn more. Where in Canada are you located? What kind of work would I do at your ranch? What animals do you have? I am 22 years old, I study Forestry, and I always wanted to visit Canada. I'm looking forward to hear back from you!

All the best, Miriam"

As emails go, not the best one that's ever been written. But I have no experience in writing emails, let alone in a foreign language, and that's all I can do for now. I float home, equally thrilled and disbelieving that I emailed a stranger about possibly living with her for a while. I'm not sure who I am any more, but I like her a whole lot better than the old me.

Over the next week, a flurry of emails goes back and forth across the Atlantic. I learn that Rose lives in 100 Mile House, a small town in central British Columbia. She has horses, chickens, cats, and a dog, and wants some help caring for the animals and "whatever else I need help with." She is vague on that subject, and I don't question her further. I'm much more interested in the people, the land, and how she got there. Rose, her late husband and her kids immigrated nine years earlier because they wanted a simpler life closer to nature. She paints a picture of cowboys riding on their horses across wide-open pastures, of friendly neighbours popping in for coffee and a chat, of fishing, swimming in lakes, and having campfires under the stars. It all sounds so amazing, I get more excited with each email I receive.

She writes in German, due to her having lived in Germany for several years before she and her family moved to Canada. When I find out that she lived only an hour away from where I grew up, I take it as a sign, and I make a decision: I will book a ticket to Canada to go to Rose's ranch for the summer.

Before I can change my mind, I head to the travel agency the very next day. I have 800 Euros saved, and hope that's enough for a ticket—I have no idea how much it could cost, and I don't have a credit card. Hesitantly, I step into the agency, my heart pounding.

A middle-aged lady looks up from her computer, and greets me with a smile. "Can I help you?"

"Yes, I would like to book a flight to Vancouver."

"Sure, no problem. Have a seat."

I plop myself down in front of her desk.

She starts to ask me several questions, none of which I have an answer to. From where do I want to fly?

Do I care if I have one or two stops, or do I prefer a direct flight?

When do I want to return?

I don't know. So, I do what I always do when I'm nervous: I start to babble.

"Uhm, I want to go in August, but I'm not sure yet for how long. I don't know anything about flying, because I've never flown before! But I've always wanted to go to Canada, and I've found a place where I can stay, and we haven't actually talked about for how long—maybe three weeks?— and I also don't know how much a ticket costs; how much is it?" I stop to take a breath, and the agent smiles patiently.

"No worries, let me explain. First, if you don't know when you want to return, you can get an open-ended ticket. That means that you pay for your return flight today, but the date is flexible. The only condition is that it has to be within a year of your departure date."

"Oh, that sounds perfect!" I say, relieved.

"Second, direct flights are usually a bit more expensive than flights where you have a stopover. It also depends on your departure airport. There are daily direct flights from Frankfurt to Vancouver, but, let's say you want to fly from Munich, you would have to stopover in Toronto."

"I don't mind if it takes longer, if that makes it cheaper," I say, in typical college-student fashion.

In the end, I book an open-ended flight for August 5th for 500 Euros. The agent tells me that I don't have to pay it right away, but I insist to make sure that I won't chicken out. I go to the nearby bank, withdraw the amount, and return, paying in cash.

Afterwards I head to the computer lab and email Rose my arrival date.

There's only one thing left to do: tell my parents.

Chapter 10

A ROCKY START

"You want to do *what*??"

"Are you crazy?"

"That's way too dangerous."

"We won't allow it."

"YOU CAN'T GO."

That's when I have enough. "I'm twenty-two, I can do whatever I want," I tell my assembled family crossly.

I have just informed the family of my summer plans, and they are not taking it well. They are all there: Mom, Dad, Grandma, Sister, Oliver. Seeing them all sitting there as a unit, ganging up on me, only shows me how right I was to do this. I need to get away from them.

"Well, you're not getting any money from us," my mother says.

"I don't need money, I have my own. I've been working for ten years, remember?" I remind her.

My grandma is concerned for my safety, picturing me stranded in the wilderness, fighting off bears and hostile Indians. I cringe inwardly at her old-fashioned stereotyping, but then again, she is 72 years old. I guess she's entitled to her old-fashioned views. I do my best to reassure her, explaining to her that I will be staying with a mother with children, "in a real house, not a teepee, Oma." When I mention that she used to live just around the corner from here, grandma is slightly mollified.

Oliver opens his mouth and begins to speak, but I cut him off. "Stay out of this. What I do is none of your concern." He turns bright-red and closes his mouth again.

Emma is quiet, and I suspect she is the only one who wants me to go. Things between us are still extremely awkward, and it's easier for her—and everyone—when I'm not around. That's why I'm so surprised at the strong opposition I get from everybody else. After all, I was gone for weeks last summer, and they didn't care. Granted, I stayed in Germany. Maybe it's the fear of the unknown? Like me, they have never been outside of Europe, and I guess that's what scares them.

At the end of this exhausting afternoon, my mother sums up the conclusion to our long, fruitless discussion in one sentence. "We don't approve of you going, but we can't stop you."

That's right.

On a Friday night in June, I find out that Emma is pregnant. It's close to 10pm, my mother went to bed already, and it's just me and my dad in the kitchen. He looks at me strangely, and I can tell that he wants to tell me something.

"What is it?" I ask.

He doesn't reply immediately. Instead, he fidgets, apparently searching for the right words. After a few moments he seems to have found them, because he straightens, looks me directly in the eyes, and says joyfully, "We found out something this week."

Dread washes over me—suddenly, I know. "Emma is pregnant?" I guess, with barely suppressed bitterness.

"Yes! How did you know? Did she tell you?" Dad asks me happily.

"Nope, just a lucky guess," I murmur. The pain is sharp, like a knife twisting in my gut. I cross my arms protectively in front of my belly, trying to soothe the pain. She is going to have *his* baby. I have a hard-enough time seeing them together, and soon they will be doting parents? I don't know if I can take it. Another thought occurs to me.

"Are they planning on getting married?" I'm silently willing my dad to say no, they are not. *Please*, just say no.

But instead, he looks at me with compassion, and nods quietly. "Yes, in August. They want the baby to have the same last name as Oliver. They are going to have a small ceremony at the town hall, just with family. I think once the baby is here, they want to have a church wedding."

"When in August?" I ask, barely above a whisper.

"On the 24th."

"I won't be here," I tell him. "I'll be in Canada."

"I know," he acknowledges quietly.

We both sit there, not saying anything.

There is nothing left to say.

Fortunately, the weeks fly by. I'm busy with school, and I take on extra shifts at the office supply store I work at to save as much money as possible.

Before I know it, the day before my departure has arrived. I've so overstuffed my backpack that it's in danger of bursting, and it's so heavy that I can barely lift it. But I'm unclear on what exactly I will be doing, or for how long I will be gone for, so I packed summer clothes, fall clothes, four pairs of shoes (sandals, runners, hiking boots, one pair of heels), all my underwear, and a couple of "date" outfits, *just* in case I meet someone. I'm also bringing three books, because I can't bear to travel without them, and mainstream E-readers are still a thing of the future. In addition to that, I packed my thick German-English dictionary, and a diary to record my adventures in.

The most superfluous item I've packed is hair dye. Yes, you heard that right. I've been dying my hair a bright auburn red for eight years, refreshing the colour religiously once a month. I'm not about to interrupt my colouring schedule just because of travel. I also packed all the toiletries I could possibly need for at least two months, my birth control pills for *three* months, two economy-size packs of tampons, and a box of condoms, just in case. Like I said, that poor backpack is *full*.

I'm too nervous to sleep that night. I toss and turn, checking the time every few minutes. We have to leave the house by 5am, because it will take us three hours to get to the airport. Despite their disapproval, my parents offered to drive me to the airport, and I gratefully accepted. I'm seriously freaked out now, and want them to be around for as long as possible.

At 2am, I give up on sleep, turn on the light and try to read. I can't concentrate, so I toss my book to the side and stare out of the window instead. Where will I be tomorrow at this time? Or next week? Am I about to make the biggest mistake of my life, or will my life change for the better? Only time will tell.

I'm too restless to sit still, so I tiptoe slowly through the house, keeping the lights off. I've lived in this house since the age of four, and I know every creaky floorboard, which step of the stairs to avoid (the fourth one from the bottom), and where the fragile, easy-to-break knickknacks are placed dangerously close to the edge. I'm in the strangest mood: scared shitless, but also hyped up and excited. I imagine it's the feeling people have shortly before stepping into thin air when bungee-jumping. The waiting is the worst, and I just want to get started on my trip.

Finally, it's 5am. Freshly showered and blow-dried, I hoist my heavy backpack into our car's trunk. The sun is rising as we drive towards Munich, infusing me with a heady feeling of optimism. The world is my oyster! It's ready for me to explore it!

Toby and Amber meet us at the airport. They promised to see me off, and I'm so happy to lay eyes on their smiling faces, I give them each a huge bear-hug. My parents head off in search of coffee, and the three of us huddle together in a corner.

"How are you feeling? You must be so excited!" Amber says, squeezing my arm.

"I'm so jealous!" Toby squeals, punching my shoulder. "Can you take me with you?"

"I wish!" I laugh, meaning it. "Can't you tag along? You, too, Amber!"

Having them here means the world to me. All my anxiety is dropping off, being replaced by excitement. Instead of feeling like a self-indulgent brat, they let me know that what I'm about to do is normal. I'm a college-student, and the time to explore and get to know the world and yourself is while you are young. I'm indefinitely grateful for their support. Them showing up today delivers a message to my parents, as well: this isn't as outlandish as they think it is. I hope they can relax a bit, and feel better about sending me off.

The good-bye is heart-wrenching. You would think I'm taking off into a war zone. My dad hugs me hard, and tells me with a wobbly voice, "Be careful, okay? Take care of yourself!"

My mom urges me, "If something is wrong, come home immediately, you hear? Don't worry about the money. Just take the next plane home!"

I have a lump the size of Mount Everest in my throat, trying desperately (and unsuccessfully) not to cry. "I will, I will," I promise them, before turning to my friends.

"Have the time of your life, kid!" Toby says, enveloping me into another bear hug. "I know you will. You will come home a changed woman!"

I hope so, I think to myself.

Amber is last to say her good-byes. "I hope you'll find what you're looking for," she says, and we embrace for a long time. She's been there for me throughout this whole mess, and knows me better than anyone else who's assembled here. She alone understands how much I'm hoping to achieve with this journey.

When I wave for the last time, I'm determined to take all their well-wishes to heart, and make them proud.

I will be a new, better person when I come back! I silently promise them. *Just wait and see.*

However, the flight isn't off to a good start. It's been eleven months since 9/11, and airport personnel is still jumpy. They find something suspicious in the cargo hold of our plane, and we are delayed by three hours. Being a virgin flier, I haven't grasped the full meaning of the delay yet. For now, all I know is that I've been stuck next to an extremely nervous flier, and that she has already exhausted me. Her coping mechanism is talking incessantly, while trying to force her "relaxing" pills on me in regular intervals. I decline every time, since I don't trust slightly unhinged strangers. Also, they don't seem to have any calming effect on her whatsoever, making me question their effectiveness.

When we finally leave, I've been up for 32 hours already. I have bypassed tiredness and moved on to being hyper. That means that suddenly, my seat neighbour Connie has been transformed from being deranged to being delightfully quirky in my eyes. We chat for most of the flight, telling each other our life stories. At some point, she mentions, "I wonder how long it will take us to get our connecting flights in Toronto," and I ask her what she means.

"Oh, because of the delay in Munich we will have missed our original flights," Connie states matter-of-factly.

This never occurred to me. "What?" I shriek. "No! Someone is waiting for me in Vancouver to pick me up!"

"They will have learnt of the delay, no worries," she tries to reassure me, her chill pills finally working. She is as calm as can be, but I'm seized by panic.

"How does this work?" I ask her. "What will happen once we have landed in Toronto?"

"You know what? That's a good question. Let's ask one of the stewardesses." She presses the call bell, and after a short time our smiling flight attendant appears.

"How can I help you?"

Connie starts asking a bunch of questions in English, none of which I can understand in my hysteria. Same goes for the answers, and I impatiently wait for them to finish their conversation to find out what the flight attendant said.

"So? What did she say?" I demand as soon as they have finished.

"There are several planes going to Vancouver today, and they will try to get us on them. Once we have landed, we will have to get our luggage, head to the domestic terminal, check our luggage back in, and then wait for our names to be called. Not all of us will be able to get on the first flight out, so we might be stuck there for a few hours."

Oh no. Oh no oh no oh no. This all sounds very complicated. Rose is supposed to pick me up in Vancouver, and what will she think if I'm not there at the appointed time? And then something else dawns on me. I never gave her my flight number. All I emailed her was the date and the arrival time. She won't know about the delay. What if she leaves again? What if I'm stranded at the airport?

The worst about it is that I can't do anything right now. I'm stuck in this metal tube in the sky, completely helpless. I turn to Connie and ask her imploringly, "Could I please have one of your pills now?" She happily complies.

Once in Toronto, chaos ensues. I have absolutely no idea what to do, so I simply follow Connie. She expertly leads me to the luggage carrousels, where we get lucky and receive our bags within the first ten minutes.

"Follow me," she calls over her shoulder, and I obediently do. We have to go from the international terminal to the domestic one, and we have two options: take a bus or walk. Connie decides to walk, and we jog along an endless corridor, with me huffing and puffing under the weight of my heavy backpack. Once we arrive, we have to line up to check our luggage again. I would be completely lost without my experienced travel companion, and I'm so grateful to her that I'm close to tears. Once our bags are checked, we line up to go through security. A stern-looking officer is going through my carry-on, and pulls out my nail file. He brandishes it angrily at me, and starts yelling at me in English. I'm dumbfounded. What does he want? What has my innocent little nail file done to him to make him so mad? He must have asked me a question, because he has stopped shouting and looks at me expectantly.

"Uhm, sorry, ah, not much English, not understand," I stammer. I can speak better than this (if not much), but given how tired and overwhelmed I am, my barely-there command of the English language has abandoned me. He shakes his head with disgust, throws the file into a box sitting next to him, and waves me through.

Once I'm reunited with Connie, I tell her what just happened. "What did he want from me?" I ask her, still clueless.

"You're not supposed to bring anything sharp on the plane," she explains.

"But they didn't say anything in Munich!" I protest, feeling stupid.

"Yeah, they should have. Maybe they didn't see it. Don't worry about it," she says distractedly. "Let's figure out where we should wait."

I trail behind Connie, my cheeks still burning. So far, I have made one blunder after another. I'm about as far removed from the confident, fearless traveller of my fantasies as I could be.

Connie purposefully marches up to a desk and asks the harassed-looking woman behind it a few questions. After a short exchange, she returns to me.

"They will call up the passengers in alphabetical order," she informs me.

"What's your last name?" I ask her. It's Braun, which will put her into the first available plane. Mine is Meier, and the chances of making it onto the same plane are slim. The thought of being left behind without my new BFF frightens me. She has become my lifeline in this new, scary world I'm finding myself in.

"You will be fine," she tries to reassure me. "Just listen to the announcements, and then follow the crowd. Seriously, you can't get lost at an airport."

I'm not too sure about that, so I'll have to take her word for it.

When they call up her name, I thank her profusely. By now, Connie seems to be eager to get away from me, and with a quick wave she hurries off.

I'm alone.

For a while, I just sit there, not moving. Then I'm suddenly seized by panic that they may have called my name and I missed it, and now I'll be stuck in this horrible airport forever. I gather all the courage I can muster, and approach the desk. In halting English, I ask the same harassed-looking woman from before if they have called my name yet. Without looking up, she shakes her head no. I want to find out if she has an approximate timeline, but I can't find the words. I slink back to my seat, and settle in to wait. Every time the overhead announcement comes on, I strain my ears, terrified I may miss it.

Finally, after an hour-and-a-half, the crackling voice says something that sounds like "*Marian Mayer.*" I jump up and speed-walk to the desk. "They said 'Miriam Meier?'" I ask, and this time the lady looks up and smiles.

"Yes, they did, dear," she says kindly, obviously feeling sorry for me. She points me into the right direction, and when I finally sink down in my seat on the plane, I breathe a deep sigh of relief.

The stress and the sleepless night take their toll, and I fall asleep almost immediately. I don't wake up until we touch down in Vancouver.

It is now 11pm. We were supposed to land at 3pm. After I have retrieved my backpack from the carrousel and gone through customs, I slowly wander around the almost-empty airport. Rose sent me a picture of herself, and I realize within minutes that nobody who looks like her is waiting for me. My heart sinks. What am I supposed to do now?

In a daze, I continue to circle the arrival lounge. Most of my fellow passengers have disappeared. There's a group of five or six guys sitting in a corner on the floor, laughing and talking. They seem to settle in for the night. I don't know what to do. Bleakly, I consider simply staying at the airport, and trying to find a flight back home the next day. I'm clearly not cut out for this.

Tears are starting to fill my eyes. Oh God, I don't want to go back home. But what else can I do?

And then, help arrives. A flight attendant who must have noticed my despair approaches me.

"Do you need help?" she asks me kindly. "You look lost."

I'm so relieved, I almost burst into tears on the spot. With some difficulty, I explain my dilemma.

"Have you tried calling your friend?" she asks me reasonably, and I have to admit that no, I haven't. It hasn't even occurred to me. I sheepishly admit as much, and she offers to make the phone call for me, apparently having decided that this is a task beyond my capabilities in my current state. She is not wrong.

I hand over Rose's phone number, and we head to a pay phone. She punches in the digits, waits for a moment, and then the call is being answered. After a short exchange that I can't follow because my brain has completely stopped working, the nice flight attendant hands the phone over to me.

"Your friend wants to talk to you," she says with a smile. I hesitantly take the receiver, and put it against my ear.

"Hello?" I say uncertainly.

"Miriam, sweetheart!" An enthusiastic voice greets me. "I'm so relieved you made it, I was so worried! What happened?" To my immense relief, Rose speaks German, which greatly simplifies our conversation. I explain about the delay and the missed connection in Toronto.

"I sent my other two exchange students to the airport to pick you up. They waited for hours, but finally they went home to Anne's uncle's house. Let me call them right away, I'll tell them to pick you up!" She instructs me to wait outside the arrivals building, and that it will take about half an hour for them to get to the airport.

My guardian angel has been waiting patiently for me to finish my call. "Everything sorted out?" she asks me.

"Yes. Thank you so, so much!" I thank her profusely, feeling much better. I don't know what I would have done without her.

"You're welcome. Good luck, and welcome to Canada!" With these words, she's off. I shoulder my heavy pack and head outside. It's a warm night, and I collapse onto the sidewalk, leaning my back against the building. The sidewalk is deserted, I'm the last straggler left. Looking up, I see the Canadian flag blowing merrily in the wind, and a big smile stretches across my face. I finally made it. It feels like I have been travelling for weeks, instead of only one day. But it doesn't matter now. I'm here!

Forty minutes later, a turquoise, beat-up Ford Escort comes around the corner. It's the dirtiest car I have ever seen, and I wonder if that's the vehicle that has come to rescue me. It slows down, and comes to a stop in front of me. The passenger door opens, and a tall girl with blond hair gets out. "Hey, are you Miriam?" she asks me in German.

"Yes, I am."

"Oh, *finally*! We had no idea what had happened to you. I'm Anne, we're here to pick you up. Let's get your stuff into the trunk."

I do as I'm told, and slide into the backseat. A young guy is sitting behind the wheel, his blond hair sticking up in all directions. He turns around, smiles, and sticks out his hand for me to shake it. "Hey, so good to finally meet you! I'm Bernd. What happened?"

As we speed off into the night, I recount my story once again. When I'm done, they tell me a little about themselves. They are both 21, from the south of Germany, and have been dating for a year. They enrolled at my college, and will start their first semester in the fall. One of the prerequisites of our school is to gain some experience in our chosen field, usually in the form of volunteer work or a practicum. They decided to do their practicum at Rose's ranch, and have been there for three weeks already.

As much as I want to find out more, I can't keep my eyes open any longer. I fall asleep, and when we arrive at our destination, I wake up just enough to make my way into the room Anne shows me. I'm back asleep the moment my head hits the pillow.

When I wake up the next morning, I feel like a new woman. Well rested, optimistic, and ready to face a day that's a complete unknown. *Exciting.* What felt scary yesterday, when it was dark and I was tired beyond words, feels like a great adventure in the light of a new morning.

I'm in a bedroom that's all pink. Pink walls, pink curtains, pink ruffles around the bed. The sun is streaming in through the pink-framed window, and I smell coffee. I jump out of bed, bemused to find myself still wearing my clothes from yesterday. I didn't realize I slept in them. Oh well, saves me getting dressed. I peek out of the door, wondering where the bathroom might be located. I try the door next to mine—bingo. I pee and brush my teeth and hair, and then I go downstairs in search of my new companions.

They are in the kitchen, eating cereal and drinking coffee.

"Good morning!" I greet them.

"Morning. Did you sleep well?" Anne asks.

"Do you want some coffee?" Bernd offers. I say yes to both, and join them at the kitchen table.

"Whose house are we in?" I ask.

"My uncle's," Anne replies. "He immigrated to Canada 20 years ago."

"How awesome!" I say enthusiastically. "How does he like it here?"

Anne makes a face. "He says he loves it, but I'm not sure. I've been here three times, and I don't think I'd like to live in Canada. People can be very superficial."

Hmm. I don't want to get into an argument with this person I just met, but her words make me bristle. How dare she insult this country I have pinned all my dreams and hopes on? I decide to let it go, and change the subject.

"What's the plan for today?"

"We are going to buy a car!" Bernd says cheerfully, and I raise my eyebrows in surprise.

"What? Seriously?"

"Yup! We have three more weeks left at Rose's place, and then we want to explore Canada for a few more weeks. The best way to do that is with your own vehicle."

"That's great!" I reply. "How much do you think it will cost?"

"Our budget is $1,000," Anne informs me. "The challenge is to find something that's halfway decent for this amount."

"We will," Bernd reassures his girlfriend. He seems to be a real optimist, and I like his sunny disposition and easy-going nature. This might just work out after all!

After breakfast, we get started on the hunt for a cheap car. We quickly learn that $1000 cars can be found at any car dealership, but that the salesmen are reluctant to let you know that. At first, they all try to sell us a more expensive one, not believing that our budget can't be expanded even a little. But Anne stays firm, which results in us being led to the back, where they keep their clunkers.

Finally, at the third or fourth dealership, Anne and Bernd settle on an old Dodge. Since none of us know much about cars, our criteria for choosing one is a simple process: does it run? Check. Does it make any funny noises? Not that we have noticed. Does smoke come out from under the hood? No. Is it comfy? Yes. Done!

Thrilled, they fork over the cash, and head to a car insurance place to buy insurance for a month.

By now it's late afternoon, and we still have a six-hour drive ahead of us to 100 Mile House. Bernd proudly settles himself behind the wheel of his new car, and Anne invites me to ride with her in Rose's Ford. I get the distinct impression that it's less of an invite, and more of a command—she clearly doesn't want me spending time alone with her boyfriend. It makes no difference to me, even though I have to admit that Bernd is easier company than his high-strung girlfriend. But to keep the peace, I willingly climb into the passenger seat next to her.

During the drive, she fills me in about life with Rose.

"She is a nice lady," Anne begins. "But she is completely unpredictable. She changes her mind all the time, and you never know what to expect. One day she will tell you how much she loves the barn, and the next she will ask you to tear it down. It's crazy!"

"What kind of work have you guys been doing?" I ask curiously.

"Well, that's another thing. Rose doesn't know what she wants us to do, so we have been trying to find stuff to make ourselves useful. She only has a few chickens and three horses there right now, no other animals except for one dog and one cat. We make sure the horses have enough water, but there isn't much else to do for them. They are on pasture and don't need feeding. We chopped a ton of fire wood for the winter, and now she wants us to bail hay. Honestly, we have no idea how to do it, we've been trying to figure it out."

She looks at me with sudden hope in her eyes. "You don't happen to know how to make hay, do you?"

I shake my head vehemently. "Not at all. Sorry, Anne."

"Aww well," she sighs. "We'll get the hang of it eventually." I lean back in my seat, watching the landscape change from lush rainforest to dry grasslands with hundreds of cattle grazing, and think to myself: this is going to be interesting.

Chapter 11

THE COWBOY

Rose couldn't be more welcoming. "Miriam, you poor thing!" she calls as soon as she sees me. "Come here," and she envelops me in a big hug and gives me a kiss right on the lips. "You finally made it, you must be exhausted!"

I am. Jet lag has caught up with me, and I'm dead on my feet. Rose shows me my room, and I collapse onto the bed, falling asleep immediately.

At breakfast the next morning, Rose announces that she wants to visit her daughter in Kelowna, and invites me to come along. Thrilled to get to see more of the country, I happily agree.

Am I imagining it, or is Anne glaring at me? As it turns out, I am not imagining it. A little bit later I overhear her bitching to Bernd that "we have been here three weeks, and Rose hasn't taken us anywhere. *She* comes along, and gets to go on a vacation right away? It's not fair."

I'm annoyed. What did I ever do to that girl? It's not my fault that Rose asked me. I would be stupid to say no just to spare Anne's feelings.

"If you wouldn't be so miserable, maybe people would enjoy spending more time with you," I mutter to myself, and then get my stuff to put it in the car.

We spend three days on the road. Rose is a gifted storyteller, and she keeps me entertained with stories about the cowboys in her neighbourhood, the rumours and intrigues, and how she ended up in Canada. She has lived an adventurous life, moving all over Europe, living on a houseboat for a while, before immigrating to the Wild West. Her husband passed away three years earlier, and she has since been living alone on the ranch with her two young kids.

Every night we stay with someone else: first her daughter, then a couple of her friends. "We help each other out," she explains to me. "I have a network of people I can crash with all over the province, and I return the favour when they come to 100 Mile House. It saves the money for a hotel, and we get to visit. Everybody wins!"

I compare this way of thinking with how I grew up. It would never occur to my parents to ask anyone for help, let alone sleep at their house. I try to remember if they ever stayed at someone's house overnight, but I come up empty—they haven't. Isn't Rose's way of life much more interesting? Much more connected?

Once we are back home, this trend continues. Rose gets frequent visitors, usually in the evenings, with neighbours and friends dropping by unannounced for a cup of tea and a chat. It's a novelty for me, and I'm fascinated. Despite her living alone—well, without a man, she does have her kids, and currently three German students for company—she doesn't appear to be lonely. She has plenty of company in her life! I understand for the first time that there are many more ways to live life than either being in a relationship, or wanting to be in one. *Interesting.*

While the evenings are relaxed, the days are often tense. It quickly becomes clear that none of us know what we are doing. Rose has about as much experience in ranching as we do, which results in the blind leading the blind. She gets frustrated with us for not being able to bring her vision to life, and we get frustrated with her for changing her mind every few days.

To avoid the tension, we stay out of her way as much as we can, and stay busy by chopping ever more wood, trying to repair fences, cleaning up the barn, and cutting hay. When it's too hot to work outside, we head to the nearby lake to cool off. I have to be careful not to appear to be interested in Bernd, because Anne watches me like a hawk. The funny thing is that I'm not interested in him at all; I simply like him. He's a nice guy, and seems, at times, the only sane person in this crazy house.

But despite the occasional temper flare-ups, I love it here. In the mornings, we watch deer come out of the woods to graze on the field behind the house. Hummingbirds visit all day long, drinking from the feeders hanging in front of the windows. Marmots are omnipresent, popping their fuzzy little heads out from rock piles, whistling loudly to each other, and scampering across the porch to eat Rose's flowers, much to her consternation. I have never seen marmots before, and I adore these little creatures with their fluffy tails and cute yellow bellies.

After I have been there for about two weeks, Rose announces one morning that yet another visitor is expected. "Richard from Vancouver is coming today. I'm going to clean the house, and you guys bale the hay, okay?"

Easier said than done. We do our best, but something isn't working right with the bailer—the bails come out looking wonky and loose, and some of them fall apart when we try to pick them up. We have to undo the strings, spread out the hay, and do it again. It's a tedious, frustrating job. We are hot, sweaty and dusty, and relieved when the sun starts to set—that means we can finally quit.

I have been so absorbed in the misery that is bailing, that I have completely forgotten about the visitor that's supposed to come. We are at the far end of the field when we notice a black truck with a camper pulling up in front of the house. Rose's car is gone, indicating that she isn't home—she has probably gone into town to buy the ingredients for dinner. Anne and Bernd are goofing off on the tractor, teasing each other and kissing, so it seems up to me to greet the stranger. *Great.* I still haven't gotten over my fear of having to speak English, and now they leave me no choice. Grumbling, I slowly make my way toward the house.

The driver has gotten out of the truck, with three children spilling out behind him. He has spotted me and walks towards me. The first thing I notice is his cowboy hat. As I get closer, I notice his eyes next: bright blue and piercing. *Gorgeous eyes,* I can't help but think. They look at me steadily, and I feel myself blush.

"Hi, are you Richard?" I call out. "My name is Miriam, I'm from Germany." Yikes, why did I just say that? That's so dumb! I cringe inwardly.

Then the stranger opens his mouth and responds in German in a deep, pleasant baritone, "I'm from Germany as well. I'm Richard." He keeps looking at me, and I can't look away; his eyes are mesmerizing. And his voice! It's like liquid, dark chocolate. Morgan Freeman, go home—a new voice is in town. It's the sexiest, most beautiful sound I have ever heard, and I want him to keep talking.

"How was your drive?" I inquire, waiting slightly breathlessly for him to open his mouth again.

"It was fine," he says, and I feel my knees go weak. Damn, what is happening here? I have never had such a strong reaction to a stranger. I inadvertently glance down, and realize for the first time how I look: old shorts, dirty legs (have I shaved today? No, I don't think I have!), the cotton sweater with the funky smell (why, *why* have I worn that old stinker today?). I'm sweaty, probably red-faced, and I have the sneaking suspicion that hay is sticking in my hair (it is).

Richard asks for a shower, and I lead him to the house, trying to inconspicuously smooth my hair down as I go. After I have shown him the downstairs bathroom, I fly up the stairs to clean myself up. I shed my dirty clothes, yank the elastic out of my ponytail and a brush through my tangled hair, and hop into the shower. While soaping up and carefully shaving my legs, I'm humming to myself. I feel inexplicably happy, and can't wait to get to know him better!

When I'm done and dressed in clean clothes (I debate for a good ten minutes if I should put one of my "date" outfits on, but in the end, I chicken out and play it safe with jeans and a tee), I go to the kitchen. While I was in the shower, Richard and his kids have unloaded some stuff from their camper, amongst them a bottle of rum, a twelve pack of Coke, and three lemons, and he is fixing drinks for everyone.

"Rose, do you have ice?" he asks her, and she gets up and checks the freezer. She pulls out two empty ice trays, and shakes her head. "Sorry, we don't."

"Remind me to give you the recipe later," he jokes, and sends one of his kids out to the camper again. She returns with a big bag of ice, and he generously fills five glasses, garnishing each with a fat slice of lemon.

"Wow, you came prepared!" I exclaim, and he turns around and smiles at me.

"Always," he says, and winks. I giggle like the silly school girl I am, but I can't help myself.

We settle in around the kitchen table and talk. At first, Rose and Richard are catching up, which is how I learn that he is married and has a fourth daughter at home.

Of course, I think to myself. A nice, good-looking guy like that is obviously taken.

I shake the thought off, deciding that I can still enjoy his company. Once they are caught up on the latest, he starts telling us about his life in Canada.

Richard loves the outdoors. He is a passionate horseman, likes to go camping and hunting, and has a hobby farm at home. He tells us about galloping on his horse through the park at dawn, about flying on tiny planes to the Yukon to go hunting, about road trips to California and fancy restaurant meals in Vancouver. He immigrated to Canada when he was twenty-five, because his life in Germany had become too suffocating for him. Oh, how I know that feeling.

He describes how his first job was at a carwash, and how miserable and cold it was. He moved in December, ten days before Christmas, and he only took the bare necessities. His only pair of winter shoes had a hole in the bottom, and his foot got wet and freezing cold every day. But he managed to work his way up, and now he runs a successful landscaping business.

I'm fascinated by his story. It's the classic self-made man tale, but it's so amazing to hear someone real tell it! I have a million questions, with the most pressing one: how can *I* do it?

I'm obviously not the only one who is enthralled by his narrative. Rose, who is sitting next to him, has put her feet on his lap. What the hell? Curious how he will react, I watch them closely. At first, he doesn't do anything, and simply ignores her feet. After a couple of minutes, he excuses himself and gets up to go to the bathroom. When he returns, he refreshes our drinks, and upon handing me mine he points to the spot next to me on the bench and asks, "Scooch over?"

Ha! Miriam-1, Rose-0. I try to suppress a triumphant smile, but I am unsuccessful. He chose me!

Rose looks sour, but she recovers quickly and gets up to start dinner. While she cooks, we talk about Canada and Germany, and I ask him a fraction of the million questions I have on my mind.

It's a great evening. When we finally go to bed, it's way past midnight, and I can't stop smiling. He's the most interesting person I have ever met.

The next morning at breakfast, Rose tells him about the machines that don't work. "I'll take a look at them," he offers.

"I show you where they are!" I quickly say, before anyone else can.

As we head out, I ask him, "Are you sure you want to fix them? They are a disaster. I think they may be beyond help."

"Oh, I have years of experience. When I was growing up, my dad would take apart the farm equipment for fun, and then make me help him put it back together. I didn't enjoy it, but it did teach me something about fixing machines."

As he hunkers down to inspect the hay bailer, I settle in next to him.

"So, you grew up on a farm?"

"Yes, I did. Dairy farm. My grandfather started it, and my father took over. They thought I would continue the tradition, but I just couldn't. Working so closely with family is …"

"…Exasperating?" I finish for him, smiling. "Aggravating? Crazy?"

He looks at me, surprised. "How do you know? Most people think it would be great."

"I grew up in a family business as well," I say, and tell him a bit about my history. I leave out the part about Oliver; somehow, it doesn't seem important enough to mention.

"That's how you ended up studying Forestry, huh?" he says, nodding understandingly.

"Yup," I say. I hesitate, and then admit, "To be honest, I don't think it's the right choice for me. But I have no idea what else to do. How did you know that you wanted to become a landscaper?"

"You know, I didn't know. If you would have told me at twenty-five that I would run my own landscaping business one day, I would have thought you're crazy. But I took every opportunity that presented itself, and that's how I ended up where I am today."

He tells me that while he was working in the carwash, someone offered him a job at a construction site. The money was better, and he was sick of getting his feet wet every day, so he jumped at the opportunity.

Then, several months later, he was driving down a street and saw two guys planting shrubs alongside it. He stopped and asked them who they were working for. They gave him the name, and that guy turned out to be not only a horticulture specialist, but he also became a close friend. He taught Richard the basics of landscaping, and introduced him to his first clients.

"I only knew two different kinds of shrubs when I designed their yard," he laughs, "but I sold the hell out of them."

I look at him thoughtfully. "You make life sound so easy," I tell him. "Weren't you scared? Wasn't it hard?"

"Of course it was," he replies. "But I knew that I wanted to stay here, and I figured that if you're not afraid of hard work, you can always find a way. You just have to talk to people, and learn from them."

"Hmm. I wish I was more like you. I would love to stay here and start over."

"If you really want to, you will find a way," he says, patting my knee. "You seem like a remarkable young woman. How old are you, anyway?"

"Twenty-two," I say.

"What, that's it?"

"Hey," I protest. "Do I look that old?"

"No, not at all," he assures me. "But you are very mature for your age. The opposite to me," he grins, "I'm very immature for my age."

"How old are you?"

"Forty-eight."

I look at him closer. He has a full beard that's a beautiful shade of silver and which told me that he must be in his forties. But his skin is mostly unlined and glowing with health, and the twinkle in his blue eyes makes him appear at least ten years younger. He also moves and talks like a much younger man, and I feel a wave of regret. I really like this man a lot—too bad that he is taken.

To remind myself of that fact, I ask him, "Tell me about your kids?"

He has four daughters: the teenage-twins and ten-year old that he brought along, and a six-year old that stayed at home with her mother. His eyes light up when he talks about his kids, and I can see how proud he is of them. My heart swells—there is nothing more attractive than a man who loves his family.

I wait for him to mention his wife, but he doesn't. I'm extremely curious about the woman who managed to get this guy, but I also don't want to spoil the special connection we have. I say nothing, and we continue to chat about other things.

Late that afternoon, he and his three girls get ready to leave. I would be immensely sad, had he not promised to return the following week with a friend of his. "My buddy Fred is coming from Germany, and he wants to go camping. We will come back here, if that's all right?"

Is it all right? You bet it is!

I can't wait to see him again.

Chapter 12

SEX UNDER THE STARS

Five days later, he returns.

"You came back!" I beam at him, and give him a big hug.

"Did you doubt me?" he whispers into my ear, and a delicious shiver runs down my spine. I squeeze a little tighter in response, and then, regretfully, let go.

Richard introduces his friend Fred, who is visiting for the first time. He is slim, of average height, with blond hair and a blond mustache. He seems to be a bit traumatized, and Richard tells me later, in private, that he got spooked in the woods.

"We were supposed to meet with a couple of my hunting buddies, but we couldn't find the meeting spot. I was so deep in the woods that I thought it's easier to jump on my horse and find them on horseback, instead of trying to turn the truck and trailer around on that narrow forest road. I told Fred to stay in the truck and wait for me, and then I took off. When I returned after an hour, the truck and trailer had been moved off the road and were jackknifed in between the trees. He was sitting in the driver's seat, with the doors locked, wild panic in his eyes. He said he had heard a noise, and thought a bear was about to attack him. His flight-instinct kicked him, and he started the truck, trying to get out. Obviously, he didn't get very far. It took me an hour to get the truck out of that mess again."

Fred may not be experienced in the wilderness, but he is a gifted guitar player. He is playing in a band, and they are regularly booked on the weekends for parties, festivals, and even the annual Octoberfest of their town. As soon as Rose hears that, she jumps into her car and drives to her neighbour to borrow a guitar.

In the meantime, we start a camp fire, the boys mix drinks, and upon her return we sit down around the fire. Fred is as good as promised: he has a clear, melodious voice, and sings some of the classics we all know:

The Beatles, Bruce Springsteen, John Denver, Neil Diamond, and Green Day's *Time of Your Life*, which I love. He can also play any song you want him to; if he doesn't know it, he picks it up by simply listening to it once or twice. I'm amazed.

The sun is setting, the first stars come out, and the fire is flickering merrily. *I'm in heaven.*

Richard is sitting across from me, and we keep looking at each other. Every time I catch him looking at me I smile, and he winks.

This is utterly, ridiculously romantic. *And insane.* But I have stopped thinking; I'm living in the moment, for once in my life. *And I'm loving every second of it.*

After a couple of hours, we are all ravenously hungry. Rose ushers us into the kitchen, where she throws a few steaks into the frying pan and starts to make a salad. Richard and I are sitting next to each other, and watching Rose prepare dinner must have given him an idea. "You three want to go camping next week, don't you?"

That's true. The week before, I mentioned that our time at Rose's ranch is coming to an end soon. Anne and Bernd are almost finished with their six-week practicum, and then they can finally go on the road trip they have planned. To my surprise, they have asked me if I want to tag along, and I was only too happy to accept. However, we have absolutely no camping equipment whatsoever, just a vague plan of "roughing it" and buying only the absolute necessities.

"You know," he says thoughtfully, "I have some stuff in my camper that you could have if you want. Pots and pans, for example? Do you want to take a look?"

Hmm, let me think about that for a minute. Do I want to get away from the crowd and have some alone-time with him? Ah, yes, please! "Sure, sounds good!" I answer eagerly. We get up and go outside.

Once outside, we are both quiet. My heart starts hammering, and I feel suddenly nervous—what now? He leads me to the camper, and I dutifully peer inside, trying to locate the pots, when he suddenly pulls me towards him and kisses me.

At first, I'm startled.

Then, I'm exhilarated.

And then I kiss him back.

"I've been wanting to do this ever since I met you," he murmurs into my hair, and happiness spreads through my body like warm, liquid honey. "Nobody has ever looked at me like you do."

"How am I looking at you?" I whisper back, gazing up at him.

"Like I mean something to you." He does, oh how he does. I feel strangely tongue-tied though, unable to put my overwhelming and confusing feelings into words, so I nod silently.

"Let's go for a walk!" he says, and takes my hand. We stroll through the night, the warm air caressing us, talking quietly, laughing, kissing.

In the middle of the field, under millions of twinkling stars, we slowly sink to the ground. Our kisses become more passionate, more urgent.

"I want to feel you," he moans, pulling my top over my head.

"Me, too," I gasp, unbuttoning his shirt. There are two unbidden thoughts in my head: *He's married!*, and *One-night-stands never lead to lasting relationships*—but then he starts kissing my breasts, and I stop thinking.

We make love under the stars. It's beautiful, confusing, romantic— and uncomfortable. When we are done, I become aware for the first time that the hay stubs of the field we are lying in are digging painfully into my back and my butt.

"Ouch," I say, sitting up and reaching to my back.

"What's wrong?" Richard asks with concern. "Did something bite you?"

"No, I don't think so," I reply. "Can you take a look at my back? It hurts."

He does, and then he bursts out laughing. "Oh God, I'm sorry," he says in between hiccups of laughter, "but your back looks like a roadmap. It's covered in red marks and scratches!"

"Great," I grumble, embarrassed. "That never happens in the movies."

"You are beautiful," he assures me, and gives me a tender kiss on the lips. "It's cold, let's move into my trailer."

He helps me up and we walk to his horse trailer, hand in hand. The trailer is empty because the horses are on the pasture. He cleans out the horse manure, puts down some hay, and then gets his sleeping bag from the truck. While he does that, I duck behind the barn and take a long, much-needed pee. *Something else they never show in the movies,* I think to myself, giggling. When I return, the trailer is ready, with Richard already lying in the sleeping bag. He opens it and invites me in. "Come here, snuggle up." I slip in next to him, and we quickly fall asleep, arm in arm.

The next morning, I learn for the first time what the infamous "walk of shame" feels like. I must admit, I don't care for it. When we show up in the kitchen, with messy hair (me) and a sheepish grin (also me), the atmosphere is loaded. Richard appears calm, but I'm embarrassed. While I don't regret what happened last night, I would have preferred to not have a judgmental audience the next morning. I excuse myself as quickly as possible, and go outside to clear my head.

Anne follows me. *Damn.*

"Where were you last night? What were you doing?" she hisses. Before I can say anything, she continues, "We were looking for you! We were worried."

That gets me going. "Come on, you weren't worried. What did you think was happening? Use your imagination."

"So, did you sleep with him?" She stares at me accusingly.

"It's none of your business," I snap back, annoyed. "But if you must know—yes. And I would do it again."

In a quieter voice, she asks, "He didn't—hurt you, did he?"

I'm appalled. "Of course not! Jeez, why would you think that?"

"Well, he's so much older! Wasn't it gross?"

I look at her with a mixture of pity and contempt. "It was the best night of my life. I really like him, and it was wonderful. For your information, I don't give a damn about how old he is."

With these words, I get up and walk away.

The rest of the day passes way too quickly. Richard, Fred, and I go horseback riding, and we laugh and chat easily. The guys recount stories from the old days, and Richard and I get to know each other better. I'm relieved that last night didn't make things awkward between us. On the contrary, we are closer than before, our conversation is effortless, and we laugh a lot. Being with him is *easy*. It feels like I have known him for years, and there is a closeness and intimacy between us that I have never experienced before.

We spend another night in the horse trailer, making love and talking into the early hours of the morning. At some point, Richard sits up, looks down at me, and says seriously, "I think I love you, Miriam. It's crazy, but I do. I think we are meant to be together."

I'm thrilled to hear that, but too unsure of my own chaotic emotions to say it back. Instead, I pull him on top of me and kiss him passionately.

Before they leave the next day, Richard and I go for a walk.

"Give me a call when you're in Vancouver, all right?" he says, scribbling his cellphone- and home numbers on a piece of paper. "I have to see you before you fly back!"

I promise that I will, and give him all my numbers in Germany: my home, dorm, and cellphone.

We hug for a long time, not wanting to let go of each other.

"I can't wait to see you again," he whispers into my ear.

"Me, too," I murmur back.

"Remember: I love you."

And with these words, he drives away.

Chapter 13
MiSSED CONNECTiONS

For the next few days, I walk around with a silly grin on my face, frequently staring dreamily into space, forgetting the world around me.

I imagine what our future together might look like: basically, like a never-ending vacation, where we go on a different adventure every day, feed each other delicious morsels of food by candlelight, and ride side by side into the blazing sunset together.

In rare moments of clarity, I know that this is just dream. It can never work out. All the odds are stacked against us: we are separated by 10,000 km, twenty-five years, four children, and one marriage. A future for us is impossible. I try to regard our time together as a sexy vacation romance, an adventure I will be able to look fondly back on in my old age.

Two days after his departure, Anne, Bernd, and I leave Rose's ranch for good to embark upon our own adventure. We are headed northwest, to the tiny fishing town Bella Coola. As luck would have it, we arrive on the day of the annual Fall Fair, and are treated to old-fashioned—but to us, novelty—events like the game horseshoes, axe throwing, logging, and contests comparing the size of homegrown vegetables and the deliciousness of home baked pies. For the kids, they erected a DIY-looking merry-go-round that is tractor-operated—as in, a guy sitting on a tractor driving in circles to pull it round and round.

I'm enchanted. It feels like we stepped back in time, and emerged in the Wild West of the 50s.

We stay several days in the Bella Coola valley, hiking through the rain forest by day, admiring the many waterfalls, and freezing our butts off at night. Our plan all along was to camp at night, to save money. It's the end of August, and we thought it would still be warm at night.

This is not so. The temperatures drop to single digits (Celsius) at night, and the clammy moisture of the forest creeps through all layers of clothing and the sleeping bag to nestle right into one's bones. It's miserable, and I barely sleep because I'm so cold. At least Anne and Bernd can snuggle together and keep each other warm, but I'm alone, with only my delicious memories of Richard's hot body to keep me company.

My suggestion of getting a motel room for the night is vetoed two to one. Another definite disadvantage of being the third wheel. However, I try to be a good sport about it, and put on another layer of clothing in an unsuccessful attempt to stay warm.

Despite the uncomfortable nights, I love the days. The forest is huge and wild and ancient, and one morning, we see a Grizzly bear mama with her three cubs. We are in the car (thank God for that), drive around a bend—and there they are, in the middle of the road in front of us. Mama Bear stands up on her hind legs, either to see us better or to look more impressive, which, if that is her goal, she is 100% successful at. She is cinnamon-coloured and enormous, her three cubs look like large teddy bears come to life, and I'm literally holding my breath at this unexpected and beautiful tableau in front of us. It's one of those special moments where you feel inexplicably grateful to be alive.

Anne and Bernd met a German lady, Trudy, before I joined them, and she invited them to visit her, should they happen to be in her neighbourhood. About a week into our trip, we purposefully drive to her place in desperate hopes of being able to have a shower—it's been a week since any of us had one, and we are sick of smelling each other. Her house is a beautiful log home, located at the edge of a lake, so Canadian it almost hurts, and when she asks us if we want to stay the night we can't say yes fast enough. A hot shower and warm bed never felt so good.

Trudy is a bit of a collector of young, stray German tourists, a phenomenon I will experience again during this trip. There are certain people who love to help struggling travellers, and they are what makes travel so magical. There's a multitude of reasons for this hobby. Some of them travelled themselves when they were younger and want to return the favours they received during their trips. It's the karmic thing to do.

Others get a kick out of it, because it blows a much-appreciated breeze of fresh air into their own stale lives.

There are also the story collectors; the do-gooders; the repenters.

I don't know into which category Trudy falls. All I know is that she also brought another German traveller home: Victoria, a quiet girl in her early 20s, who is blond, buxom, and my saviour.

By now, I'm eager to get away from Anne and Bernd. As much as I appreciate that they took me along, I have the urgent need to move on. And I'm pretty sure that they feel the same way. The whole couple + one dynamic is wearing thin, and we are all ready to part ways.

Victoria is one of those girls that's a study in contradictions. She is shy, yet she travelled by herself to Canada. She looks like a German milk maid, with rosy skin and her blond hair in braids, yet has a surprisingly raucous laugh. She also knows someone in Vancouver who offered her a place to stay, and when she hesitantly asks if any of us would be interested in coming with her, I jump at the chance. To my relief, Anne and Bernd decline, and we part ways the next day.

Victoria has another likeable quality: she appreciates food, and doesn't mind spending a bit of extra money on something delicious. I'm by no means a foodie, but after a week of raisin bran cereal (which I hate, but it was two against one—*again*) and the cheapest bread we could find with bologna—no butter or mayonnaise—I'm in dire need of some fresh, colourful food.

We take the Greyhound to Vancouver, which takes the better part of the day, and provides ample opportunity to get to know each other better. Victoria is wholesome. She loves to knit, she goes to church every Sunday, and she is obsessed with blueberries. She can talk about her love for blueberries for a surprisingly long time, and I let her, happy to have found a new travel companion. If that's the price to pay, I gladly pay it.

She called her friend Alice in Vancouver before we left, who offered to pick us up at the Greyhound station.

When we arrive it's dark, and I'm grateful to Alice for waiting there for us. The Greyhound station is in a sketchy area, with some unsavory characters lingering around who look like druggies at best, and rapists at worst.

I didn't really have a mental picture of Alice, but she isn't at all what I expected. I assumed that Alice would be young, in her twenties or thirties, and I'm surprised when Victoria waves at a trim, petite woman with grey, short hair who looks to be at least sixty years old. She is dressed in slacks and a blazer, and looks decidedly out of place in this environment. She is totally at ease, unafraid of the guys lurking in the shadows, and she has such a commanding presence as she is standing next to an old station wagon that nobody dares to approach her.

Nobody but us, that is.

Alice is not a hugger, but a hand-shaker, and when she gives me a thorough once-over, I hope fervently that my clothes are clean and that I don't have dirt under my fingernails. She has a principal-like aura about her, and I'm not in the least surprised when she tells us that she used to be a teacher. This impression is further confirmed when Alice keeps correcting Victoria's pronunciation. "It's 'v ae nk – OO – v er', not 'w aen koo ver'," she tells her, and then makes Victoria say it six times, until she is satisfied.

I sit quietly in the backseat, making myself as invisible as possible. I hate being lectured.

Her governess tendencies aside, she is a nice lady, if quite unusual.

She tells us how she met her husband: he was hitch-hiking, late at night, and she stopped and offered him a ride. (A stranger. At night. *A man*. Like I said, Alice is unusual. Or crazy—you be the judge.)

They had a long political discussion bordering on an argument, and by the end of the ride, he had asked her out.

They got married three months later, but each kept their own place, only meeting up two or three times a week.

It's very different from what I've been exposed to in my sheltered life thus far. I'm learning a whole lot about relationships on this trip.

Alice is yet another collector of travelling young German girls, having a guest waiting at the house for us: Tamara, also young and blond. I'm the lone (dyed) redhead in this sea of blond girls I've encountered so far, and I feel that I stick out like a sore thumb. Well, there's nothing I can do about it.

Tamara is pleasant, despite having an impressive case of resting bitch face, and for the next week, the three of us explore Vancouver: we wander through historic Yaletown and scenic Stanley Park, three tourists amongst thousands; we eat Dim Sum in Chinatown, the *only* three white faces in a restaurant full of Chinese. The waitress' English is almost as poor as mine, which makes me feel profoundly fond of her.

We explore the popular Granville Island Public Market, intoxicated by the smells, colours, and tastes. I try cranberry wine for the first time, eat a spicy Thai curry that makes my eyes water, and Victoria is satisfying her obsession with blueberries by buying them in as many varieties as she can: dried, candied, covered with chocolate, as a smoothie, muffin, popover, and, of course, in their original form.

Alice takes us to the Lynn Valley suspension bridge, a virtually unknown little sister to the hugely popular—and heavily populated—Capilano Suspension bridge. It gives you the same fear-fuelled adrenaline kick, minus the people (or the hefty entrance fee).

We spend an entire afternoon in the Lighthouse Park in ritzy West Vancouver, where there are trees so gigantic, the three of us combined can't reach around them.

It would be a beautiful week, if it weren't for one giant fly in the ointment: I can't reach Richard. Despite knowing that there can't be a future for us, I'm dying to see him again. I can't stop thinking about him, and he *did* give me his cell-and home-numbers. I try to call his cell at every opportunity I can: from every payphone I come across, and once, early in the morning, from Alice's phone.

I don't get a hold on him. Half the time, a computerized female voice is saying something to me in English that I can't understand. The other half, I don't get through. Admittedly, I'm unclear about how the phone system operates, and can't figure out how the long-distance versus local calls work. I also mix up the area code with the country code, unnecessarily (and wrongly) adding two zeros in front of the number he gave me. Long story short: it's not working.

I reluctantly face the possibility that he must have given me a fake number. The more I think about it, the more it makes sense. Obviously, he wouldn't give me the right number—he is married!

I'm hurt, but I try to tell myself that it's for the best.

Not being able to connect with Richard has put a huge damper on the last few days of my trip. I try to enjoy Vancouver, but I'm failing miserably. We are all relieved when the day of my departure dawns—I wasn't much fun to be around for my two blond travel companions. I apologize profusely for being a Debbie Downer, and thank Alice for her hospitality.

It's a grey, overcast day, perfectly matching my mood. Staring out of the window of the cab on my way to the airport, watching the city whiz past me, I reflect on the past six weeks.

I met new people, experienced the most romantic romance of my life, saw bears, ate sushi for the first time, slept in a car, under the stars, and in five different bedrooms.

Canada has captivated me. The famous kindness and helpfulness of the Canadians is not a cliché, but the truth, and I fondly think back to the flight attendant who saved me on the day I arrived and was stranded at the airport; to every person in Vancouver who gave us directions when we looked lost; to Rose, Trudy, and Alice, who took me in, gave me a bed to sleep in, shared their food, and showed me that life can be lived in many more ways than what I thought possible.

My thoughts return to Richard. Despite the seemingly obvious, I still can't believe that he lied to me. Am I such a poor judge of character? He seemed so sincere. He looked me in the eye and told me he loved me. I refuse to believe that I imagined our chemistry—our connection was *real*. You can't fake that! Or can you? Did he?

After I check my luggage at the airport, I wander around, unwilling to go through security just yet. I did tell him the day of my departure—maybe he's here? Ignoring the loud voice in my head telling me I'm ridiculous, I walk in large circles, keeping my eyes peeled for bright blue eyes, a silver beard, and a cowboy hat. Every time I see one of those hats, my heart skips a beat—followed by the disappointing realization that it isn't him.

Finally, I have to go through security if I don't want to miss my plane. I take one last look around, before declaring defeat.

As I'm flying away from the country—and the man—I fell in love with, I try to convince myself to be grateful for having had an amazing adventure, instead of grieving what wasn't meant to be.

I'm unsuccessful.

Chapter 14

REUNION

Being back home feels strange. I try to tell my parents of my experiences, and how it changed me, but I can't find the words. Besides, I'm sure they won't get it. How can I explain that I'm a changed woman? That I have glimpsed a bigger world beyond the small one I have known until now? That other people have left their country, to start fresh somewhere else? *That I want to be one of them?*

I only have one week left before the new semester starts, and I'm keeping busy doing laundry and packing. On the second day of being back, I decide to bake a cake. Baking usually calms me down, and I'm so restless, I'm in desperate need of some calming down. I'm vigorously beating the dough (by hand, to work off some of my nervous energy), when the phone rings. We don't have caller ID, so I have no idea who the caller is.

Sighing, I put the spoon down and head to the stationary phone in the corner.

"Miriam Meier," I say upon picking up. It's our custom to always announce our full name when answering the phone.

"Miriam?"

"Yes, who is this?"

"It's me!" Pause. I hate when people do that. Who is "me"? He answers my unspoken question with one word: "Richard."

I'm so stunned, my knees give out and I have to sit down. I slide onto the floor, the phone clutched tightly to my ear, not knowing if I can believe what I just heard.

"Richard?" I whisper. "Is it really you?"

"Yes," he says clearly, and I finally recognize his beautiful, deep voice.

"Oh God, I can't believe I'm finally talking to you," he exclaims. "Why didn't you call me? I was waiting for you to give me a call!"

"I tried!" I protest. "Your number didn't work! I thought you had given me a fake number."

"I would never do that," he says quietly. "I miss you so much."

"I miss you, too," I reply, and tears are filling my eyes.

I recount my failed attempts of trying to reach him, and we come to the conclusion that our missed connection was due to a combination of spotty cell reception where he was working during that week, and my difficulty grasping the Canadian phone system.

"You know what I did?" he says. "On the day of your departure, I went to the airport looking for you. I didn't know what time your flight was, so I stayed there for six hours."

"What?" I exclaim, surprised. "I kept looking for you, but I didn't see you!"

"I was there," he assures me. "From eight in the morning until two in the afternoon."

"That's weird," I say. "I should have seen you, I arrived just before nine."

It takes us another few minutes before realization dawns on me. "Did I tell you that I was flying via Toronto?"

Silence. Then: "No, you didn't. I was in *international* departures, thinking you would fly directly to Germany."

Damn my inexperience when it comes to travel.

We talk for an hour, telling each other repeatedly how much we miss one another.

"I have to see you," he says eventually. "Can I visit you?"

"You mean *here*?" I say, disbelievingly. "In Germany?"

"Yes. Do you want me to come?"

"Of course I do!" I blurt out, jubilantly.

He tells me that it will take him about four weeks to organize his work before he can leave. Four weeks is nothing compared to my fear that I would never see him again. I'm *ecstatic*.

From then on, we talk on the phone every single day. Having only spent three days together, we get to know each other during those phone calls. We recount our days, tell each other about our lives, and share our worries. I feel closer to him than to any of my friends—he's the best friend I never had until now.

The one thing we don't do is make any big plans. Beyond knowing that he will be here soon (he booked his ticket), I have no idea what we will do once he's here, but I decide to worry about it later. That's future Miriam's problem!

Before I know it, the day of his arrival dawns. We decided that I'll pick him up from the airport in Frankfurt, so we can spend a night together before he drives to his parents. He's going to visit them for a few days before returning to me.

What to wear? I've been fretting about this question for days. In the end, I decide on a short skirt, platform heels, and my faux leather jacket. I hope to convey a sexy, confident vibe. Besides, what guy doesn't like short skirts?

The airport is four hours away, which means that I have to get up at 4 a.m. I take a shower, blow-dry my hair carefully, pack an overnight bag, and then I'm off.

The entire drive I'm pivoting between over-the-moon excited to wanting-to-throw-up nervous. My heart is pounding furiously, even though it's still hours before I'll see him.

My thoughts go in circles, asking the same questions over and over:

What if he's awful?

What if he thinks *me* awful?

What if I find him unattractive?

What if he finds *me* unattractive?

What if sex will be terrible?

What if, what if, what if.

It's a relief when I finally arrive at the airport. The hubbub is distracting, and while my butterflies go into overdrive, the maddening thoughts are being drowned out by the noise and activity around me.

I head to the arrivals lounge, and position myself close to the escalators where the passengers will come down.

I wait.

And wait.

And wait some more.

And then, after what feels like three lifetimes, I see a cowboy hat. Is that …?

My gaze travels down a few inches, and my eyes find his. We look at each other, and a huge grin spreads over his face, matching mine. His blue eyes give me a once-over, and he nods appreciatively. Happiness floods me, in one big, all-consuming wave. I rush towards him, into his waiting, outstretched arms, and the world around us fades away.

"You are here," I murmur into his shoulder. "You are finally here."

"I've missed you so much," he whispers into my ear.

We hug for a long time. Finally, we let go, and he steps back to look at me properly.

"You look beautiful," he says.

"So do you," I tell him, meaning it. He is wearing jeans, boots, a plaid shirt, a vest, and his trademark cowboy hat. I drink in his face, those gorgeous blue eyes, the silver beard, the crinkles around his eyes.

"You are doing it again," he says.

"Doing what?"

"Looking at me in your special way. Nobody ever looks at me like you do."

"Good," I laugh, and then I add, "Come on, let's get out of here."

If I was worried that it would be awkward between us, there was no need. Our conversation flows as easily as it always does, and my nerves are forgotten. When we settle into my car, I turn to him expectantly and ask, "Where to?"

"The closest hotel," he says decisively.

I have no idea where the nearest hotel is, but I figure it can't be far. I start the car and head off randomly.

Fifteen minutes later, we pull into the parking lot of the "Hotel Post." When we approach the check-in desk, I'm suddenly shy. What will the clerk think of us? Checking into a hotel mid-day, in the middle of the week, suddenly seems seedy. "Normal" people should be at work. I self-consciously pull on my skirt, trying to make it longer.

Luckily, Richard is as calm as ever. He requests a room, and doesn't flinch when the clerk asks him (with, I'm convinced, a smirk) if he would prefer a room with a double bed or two singles?, but simply replies pleasantly, "Double, please."

When we're finally done and the door of the elevator closes behind us, I'm bright red in the face and squirm with embarrassment.

"What's wrong?" Richard asks me with genuine puzzlement.

"What do you think the clerk is thinking of us?" I fret.

"Who cares?" he replies. "We'll never see him again. Besides, he has seen much worse than the two of us, believe me."

I nod, not convinced, but trying to push past the awkwardness I'm feeling.

However, it only intensifies when we enter the room. What now?

It's been almost two months since we last slept together, and we've only done so under the forgiving cover of night. Standing in front of each other in a hotel room, in the harsh light of day, is a completely different story. I'm self-conscious, once again regretting wearing a short skirt and heels. I look anywhere but at him, until he gently lifts my chin up, looks at me, and says, "Are you nervous? Because I certainly am."

I laugh, relieved. "Yes, I'm *so* nervous. It's weird! I mean—it's you and me!"

"Let's sit down, relax." He gestures towards the corner to the couch and easy chair, and I plop onto the couch, taking off my shoes and tucking my legs under me.

Richard rummages through the mini-bar, emerging with two tiny bottles of rum and a can of coke.

"Let's have a drink," he says, pouring us each a rum and coke. He hands me my glass and sits down next to me.

"Cheers," we say in unison, clinking glasses and each taking a sip.

He looks at me.

I look at him.

And suddenly, we are all over each other, kissing frantically, tearing each other's clothes off. We stumble to the bed, not breaking apart, and dive under the sheets.

Our nerves are forgotten.

We spend all afternoon in bed, making love, dozing, talking, and laughing.

In the evening, we are starving, and we get dressed and venture out of the hotel in search of food. We find an Italian restaurant on the corner, not even five minutes away, and we go inside.

I feel like I have stepped into a different country. Italy exploded all over this restaurant, with every cliché imaginable. Red-and-white checkered tablecloths? Check. Candles stuffed into wax-covered old wine bottles? Check. Effusive mustachioed, big-bellied waiter who calls us "Monsignor" and "Bella Signorina"? Check.

I look around in wonder. From the ceiling hang hundreds of dusty wine bottles, interspersed with coils of garlic and twinkly lights. The mouth-watering aroma of garlic, tomato sauce, and warm bread scents the air.

We are seated at a cozy table in the corner, and Richard orders a bottle of Chianti. When it comes to the perfect romantic place for a date, we hit the jackpot. I'm in heaven.

We gorge ourselves on garlic mussels in white wine sauce, grilled chicken parmigiana, and shrimp Alfredo. Our waiter Luigi compliments us on our food choices, compliments Richard on his hat, compliments me on my beauty. He is completely over the top, and I love it.

We order a second bottle of Chianti, and stay at the restaurant until it closes. We are so immersed in ourselves that we don't notice anything around us—we are in a happy bubble, only punctured occasionally by Luigi and his gushing, attentive service.

The next morning after breakfast, I drive Richard back to the airport. He's going to rent a car and drive to his parents to visit them for a few days. He promises to see me as soon as possible, and we part ways.

Three days later, he arrives at my dorm. Helen, my roommate, knows about our holiday romance turning into more (fingers crossed), and she's hanging around to get a look at him, despite my pleas to leave our apartment.

"I want to see the guy you're so crazy about!" she says determinedly, and I give up.

When she gets that look in her eyes, there's no arguing with her.

I meet Richard at his rental car, a snazzy Audi A3, and warn him about Helen.

"She's nosey and opinionated, and honest in a way that offends people. Whatever she says, don't listen to her," I tell him.

Good thing I did. Helen takes one long, appraising look at Richard, and then, as I show Richard my room, grips my arm and pulls me into the kitchen before I can close the door.

"He's so old," she hisses. "What are you doing with a guy that old? Eww."

"It's none of your business," I say sharply, and then extricate myself from her grip, slamming the door to my room.

"She doesn't approve?" Richard asks.

"Don't listen to a twenty-one-year old divorcee," I fume. "She doesn't exactly have a stellar track record with men."

I sink down on my narrow single bed, and look around.

"I don't think we can stay here. It's too small, and Helen will drive us nuts. What should we do?"

Richard looks thoughtful. Then he asks me, "Have you ever been to Spain?"

Chapter 15

DO WE DARE?

A week later, in early November, I'm lying in a bikini by the pool of our hotel in the south of Spain, sipping a cold drink.

I can't believe how easy life can be.

After Richard asked me if I had ever been to Spain (no), he said next, "Then let's go!"

"Huh?" was my response. What did he mean, "let's go"? Didn't we have to make preparations, like booking hotels, researching the country, buying travel guides and reading them for weeks, before even *contemplating* going on vacation? Despite my recent six-week trip to Canada, I was still a travel newbie.

When I voiced my concerns to Richard, he laughed and shook his head. "We have a car and I have a credit card. It's the slow season, so it will be easy to find accommodations." He spread his arms wide. "What else do you need?"

What else indeed. I figured I could blow off classes for a week, and begged my boss at my part-time job to give me the week off. He, a middle-aged guy with a wife and two children, was easygoing and funny, and seemed to enjoy living vicariously through his young, mostly college student-employees. He made me promise to tell him every detail, and when I did, he gave me the time off.

The very next day, after an uncomfortable night in my single bed, we took off.

We drove through Liechtenstein, Switzerland, and France, staying in a shady motel off the highway, frequented by big, tough-looking truckers only. You know the scene in movies when the unsuspecting, hapless hero walks into the wrong bar, and it gets real quiet? That's what it felt like when we walked into the restaurant attached to the motel. I held on to Richard's hand tightly, and insisted that he stay with me at all times, even walking me to the bathroom and waiting outside. It was scary.

The next day, we drove past Avignon and Nimes, cities I had fond memories of, having spent ten days there as a seventeen-year-old as part of a school trip. Aix-on-Provence, another city close by, was where I first learnt to drink—and appreciate—wine, a gift bestowed upon me I'm still grateful for today.

On day three, we crossed the border to Spain, and as the temperature steadily climbed, we steadily shed layers of clothes. The Audi had a sun roof, and I opened it, letting the warm sun caress my bare shoulders.

And the entire time, we talked. There's nothing like those first few magical weeks in a new relationship. And we didn't even know if what we had was a relationship! All we knew was that we were crazy about each other, and wanted to know *everything* about the other person.

We talked, ate, and made love, with the lovely Spanish countryside whizzing past our windows.

We saw wild horses, thousands of flamingoes, and would stop in tiny Tapas bars when we got hungry.

We felt like we were the only two people in the world. Nothing else mattered. Our normal lives were suspended indefinitely, and I would have been happy to keep driving with Richard until the end of our days.

Now it's November, and we decided to stay in this hotel for a few days to relax from all the driving. Richard has called the airline to push the date of his return flight back by a week, and I have called my boss and told him I wouldn't be back for a few more days. I thank my lucky stars that he's so understanding.

Richard and I lie by the pool, soaking up the sun, not speaking for the moment. I'm almost dozing off when he props himself up on his elbow and looks down on me.

"What do you want to do, pretty girl?"

I open one eye, shading it with my hand against the sun. "Nothing—just stay right here, like that, with you."

"That's not what I mean. What are *you and I* going to do?"

He looks at me expectantly. "I'm all in if you are. What we have is too precious to waste. I don't want to live without you anymore."

I sit up properly, staring at him. "But what about your marriage? What about your kids?"

"You know that my wife and I haven't been happy in a very long time."

I do know. Richard has told me the story of the two of them: before he met her, he'd had three serious relationships—and a lot of flings. He was a disco fan, going out four, five times a week to dance, and often taking a girl home. His twenties flew by in this fashion, working hard and playing hard, and before he knew it, he woke up one day and was thirty years old.

He panicked. He always knew he wanted a family and children, and he realized he better start looking for a wife.

He found her back home, in Germany. Having dated lots of Canadian girls, and girls from all over the world, finding her was literally like coming home. He was on vacation for two weeks, and after that he returned to Canada.

Three months later, she came to visit. They went sightseeing, Richard showed her his favourite spots, and they talked about their goals for the future. Having children was important to her, too.

What do you need for a marriage? A big, passionate romance? Richard had had them before, and the relationships didn't last.

Wasn't it more important to have the same vision for the future? The same values? A common cultural background?

Unlike all the other girls from the past five years, she could talk to his parents, speaking the same language. That was important to him.

He broached the subject of marriage.

She was listening.

It was a bit insane, but that's what made it exciting! An adventure! Adrenaline was pumping, endorphins were running high, and they decided they would go for it. Why not?

She went home after a month, to start planning the wedding.

They had spent less than six weeks together.

Once the wedding train is rolling, it's difficult to stop it.

You don't want to disappoint your family.

You may start to doubt your decision, but what if that's a normal reaction? Doesn't everybody have doubts? It is a big commitment, after all.

People assure you that you have wedding jitters. Getting cold feet is normal. They make jokes about it, and you laugh along shakily, hoping they are right.

The wedding day is a blur of smiling faces, too many drinks, of smiling and dancing and being hugged by people until your entire body aches.

She looks beautiful.

And then, married life starts. You scraped together every penny you have to buy a house. The bachelor basement suite you lived in won't cut it for a young bride. You take every job you can get to afford the mortgage. Interest rates are at an all-time-high of 23%, and you're struggling to make ends meet. You work weekends, you take on a second job to work at nights, and the first year of marriage passes in a blur of exhaustion.

The second year rolls around. You find out that your wife is pregnant. You are overjoyed!

When you find out that she is expecting twins, you can't believe your luck.

Your girls are born, and you fall in love. So *this* is what people were talking about. This love is so deep and special, you have never felt anything like it before.

Four years later, another daughter is born.

And then, another.

You have realized a long time ago that you and your wife don't love each other. But look at everything you have achieved together! Look at your beautiful girls, your nice house, the life you have created together.

Occasionally, after too many drinks, you will confide in your best friend that you are not in love with your wife. He will respond, "Who is?"

He will then proceed to point out everything you have: four healthy, gorgeous children. He will remind you of what a good mother she is.

"Look at your life," he will say. "You have great friends," here he points at himself and you laugh, "you have your horses, your hobbies, a successful business. What more do you want?"

Love, you think to yourself. Romance. But you will nod your head in agreement, and have another drink, because maybe you want too much.

Richard is still looking at me.

"I don't want to live without you either," I tell him, reaching over to stroke his cheek. "But you will have to get a divorce! And what about your kids?"

"Believe me, the thought of hurting them is almost killing me. But they know that we are not happy, at least the twins do. They have heard us fight countless times. I think that ultimately, they will be better off when their parents are happy. Just think about it: what kind of example are we setting? I wouldn't want any one of my girls stuck in an unhappy relationship. Life is too short.

And what about us? What we have is special. I have never felt like this before! Have you?"

I shake my head. "Never."

"Miriam, we only have one life to live. We should give it our best shot, enjoy the hell out of it, and accept every gift that is offered to us. What you and I have is a gift. If we don't take it, we might regret it for the rest of our lives. I know I will."

"I would too," I tell him, and then break into a wide smile. "I'm in!"

For the rest of our vacation, we discuss how we will do this. After all, there is the small problem of us living on opposite sides of the globe.

And my school.

And him having to move out of his house.

We make a pact: when he gets home, he will tell his wife. I will talk to my parents. He will find us a place to live, and I will come to Canada as soon as possible.

I will drop out of college. The relief I feel at the thought of finally giving up Forestry is overwhelming. I have no idea what else to do, but there are more pressing matters at hand right now.

The thought of having to hurt the people we love is terrifying. We keep coming back to it, trying to think of ways to make it easier for everyone.

There aren't any. Not unless we give up on us, and return to our separate lives. And we can't bear that thought.

On our last day, we are in a somber mood. We cling to each other, trying to soak up each other's strength for what lies ahead. "I wish you could come with me," I say for the tenth time.

"Me, too," Richard says, pulling me tight. But he has his own harrowing task ahead of him. He will return to his parents, and then fly back in two days, and he is going to talk to his wife as soon as he's home.

I will speak to my parents on the same day, so it feels like we are doing it together.

Saying goodbye to Richard is impossibly hard. My eyes fill with tears, and I don't want to let him go. The last two weeks have been magical. I've never felt so complete with another person. Just him and me is enough! I don't want to enter the normal world again, filled with other people, opinions, and struggles.

"We will talk on the phone every day," he promises. "You will be with me soon."

Chapter 16

US AGAINST THE WORLD

Three days later, heart pounding, I set off to my parents' house. It's a three-hour drive, and it's the worst drive of my life. I'm so scared, I have to stop twice to throw up. My hands won't stop shaking, and I'm almost crying with fear. How will they react? Not well, that's for sure.

What parent would be thrilled if their twenty-two-year old daughter announced that she's dropping out of college to move halfway across the world to live with a married father of four? Not to mention that he's twenty-five years older, which is almost an aside compared to everything else.

Will they yell? Cry? Slap me? Anything is possible.

When I arrive, I can't get out of the car. I'm glued to my seat, my hands clasping the steering wheel so tightly my knuckles turn white. I sit there for what feels like an eternity, frozen to the spot, nauseated and paralyzed by fear. I never understood that phrase—*paralyzed by fear*—until today. It's a real thing.

I want to call Richard for moral support, but it's the middle of the night in Canada. Damn the time difference!

I close my eyes and give myself a little pep talk. "It's one bad day," I mutter to myself. "One bad day in exchange for a lifetime of happiness. You can do this."

I picture Richard, his kind blue eyes looking at me with so much love, and that gives me strength.

My limbs unfreeze, and with a deep breath, I open the car door and get out.

They are in the kitchen. Knowing that I was coming home, but unaware that I'm about to shatter their world, they are relaxed, happy to have finished their long work week. They are drinking coffee and look up as I enter the room, smiling at me. When they see my face, the smiles are replaced with frowns of worry.

"What's the matter?" Mom asks.

I can only imagine how I must look: deathly white, wild-eyed, and shaking.

"I have to tell you something," I start, and then burst into tears.

"Hey, what is it? Did something happen?" they urge.

"Y-y-yes," I stutter, and then blurt out, "I want to move to Canada."

Silence.

I plow on, "Richard and I love each other, and I want to live with him. I mean, he wants me to live with him. We both want to. I'm not happy here, and he makes me happy. *So* happy. I have to do this." I stop to take a breath, and they both stare at me, stunned.

"What?" Dad says.

"Isn't he married?" Mom asks. "And what about school?"

So far, there hasn't been any yelling and no slapping—which might only be because I'm careful to stay out of arm's reach. But I take it as a good sign, and continue a little bit calmer.

I explain how unhappy I have been over the last two years. I pointedly mention Oliver.

I also tell them that Forestry is the wrong choice for me, and that dropping out of college is not the end of the world. People do it all the time!

When they mention that "we are not quitters," I say I'd rather study something I like than being stuck in a job I hate.

But the real elephant in the room is Richard. His age. His being a father of young kids. Not to mention the fact that he is married.

They can't believe I'm so gullible. "He will never leave his wife," Mom states. "Guys never do. Not to mention his kids."

"I don't want him to leave his kids!" I protest fiercely. "He's the dad, he will still take care of them. But he isn't happy with his wife! And neither is she! They will both be better off when they get a divorce."

My parents try to talk some sense into me. Try to convince me that they are right, and I am wrong. After all, what does a twenty-two-year old know about men? About life?

We talk for hours. Going around and around in circles, neither party giving an inch. By the end of it, we are exhausted. I can tell that they are frustrated, disappointed, and mystified. They don't understand what got into their daughter. What happened to the dutiful, conscientious girl they raised? The one who would see things through, did what was expected of her (if under protest), and was, if anything, a bit *boring*?

I hate to disappoint them. All I ever wanted was their approval. I want them to be proud of me.

But I want happiness more. Having gone through the hardest time of my life has taught me that you can't take happiness for granted. If you get a chance at it, you must grab it with both hands. Don't let it slip away out of a misguided sense of obligation. Obligation to what?

To a family business they don't need me for? They have Oliver for that.

Obligation to a career choice that I already know is wrong for me? Going through with it despite this knowledge would be wrong. It's like marrying someone you don't love, and hoping you might fall in love later. It rarely happens, and sooner or later it will break apart, causing much more damage and hurt than it would have in the beginning.

I'm at a crossroads. My parents want me to go down the path they chose: the path of doing what is expected of you. Duty over happiness. But having to base your entire life on a choice you made when you were eighteen years old seems insane to me. Particularly when the choice was made haphazardly, with no real thought put into it.

I want to explore the other path. The one that leads into the unknown. The one that your head says no to, but your heart—your heart clearly tells you to go for it.

As I'm lying in bed, I call Richard. "I did it. I told them!" It's only now sinking in, and I'm giddy with relief. "Have you talked to …?"

"Yes."

"How was it?"

"Hard. Awful. But I'm glad it's done. I'm sleeping in the TV room until I find us a place. When can you come?"

"I'm going to the travel agency on Monday and see how soon I can get a flight. I love you."

"I love you, too."

After I have delivered my huge news to my shocked parents, I flee to the safety of my dorm. Figuring that going to classes makes no sense at this point, I stop going and get a second job instead. It's Christmas season, and the nearby German Post processing plant is looking for workers. The pay is spectacular: 14 Euros an hour, which is twice as much as what I'm getting at my other job.

My plan for the last few weeks in Germany is simple: earn as much money as possible, keep my head down, and lose some weight. Losing weight is an ongoing project in my life, one I regularly make resolutions along the lines of, of "This time, I'm *really* going to do it."

I also talk to Richard every single day. On some days, he's the only person I talk to, because most of my co-workers are Turkish, and they speak in their own language amongst each other.

I only tell my closest friends about my plans. Amber is supportive, even though I can tell that she isn't 100% on board. But she wants me to be happy, and she reminds me that I can come back in case it doesn't work out.

One night, I meet Toby at the pub for a beer and tell him everything: about Richard's and my romance, our trip through Spain, my decision to quit college (for now) and Forestry (forever), and my impending move to Canada. He is thrilled. To him, it makes perfect sense, because why wouldn't one follow their heart?

"We have to throw you a going-away party!" he says enthusiastically, and won't listen to my protests.

On the last Friday before Christmas, he tells me sternly to show up at his dorm's community room.

"Don't even think of bailing," he warns me, and I reluctantly comply. I've been hiding myself away from my fellow students, because I'm afraid of their judgment.

When I walk in at eight o'clock, I'm stunned by all the people that have shown up. The large room is crowded, and everybody cheers when they see me.

I'm completely overwhelmed, and as soon as I find Toby, I flee to him, out of the spotlight.

"How did you get so many people to come?" I ask him. "Did you pay them?"

He laughs and shakes his head. "No, dummy. I don't know what you're so worried about—most people think what you're doing is awesome! Just go and talk to them, they won't bite. You can get me if they're mean to you."

And with a gentle push, he shoves me towards a circle of my old girlfriends.

"Are you really moving to Canada for love? That's so romantic!"

"What an adventure, I wish I could do that."

"You're so brave!"

Toby was right; they're way more supportive than I ever thought possible. I'm surrounded by girls who want to know everything about my guy, about Canada, and what I think my new life will be like. They don't think that I'm ruining my life—they admire that I grab life by the balls.

I love the party. Toby bought a friendship book, one of those books where people share their favourite music, books, hobbies, stuff like that, and it includes a section for well wishes.

The book is almost full, and later that night in bed, I read what everybody has written.

I'm touched by the kind and thoughtful words my friends have shared with me, and bemused by a recurring theme of me being brave. Repeatedly, they comment on my courage to go for it.

Brave? Me? I want to laugh. Don't they know how scared I am most of the time?

But then, a thought occurs to me: maybe courage isn't the same as fearlessness.

Maybe, being brave means doing it *despite* the fear.

Maybe, just maybe, I'm braver than I thought?

I fall asleep with a smile on my face.

For Christmas, my parents give me a big red suitcase, their way of demonstrating that they want to support me. I love them for it, knowing that they don't agree with my choice. They also repeatedly tell me that I can come home any time. Just like back in the summer, when I travelled to Canada for the first time, they emphasize that should I run out of money, they will fly me home.

This Christmas is much more harmonious than I expected. We seem to have reached an unspoken agreement that we don't want to spoil our last few days together by fighting.

Emma and I are on speaking terms again, and not even Oliver bugs me. On the contrary, I'm almost grateful to him now. Without him, I would never have met Richard! I'm so looking forward to the next chapter of my life, that I'm in a warm, forgiving mood, loving everything and everybody.

And then, the morning of my departure dawns grey and cold. This time, only my dad drives me to the airport. The mood is subdued; we are both quiet, lost in our thoughts.

Saying goodbye to him almost breaks my heart. He has tears in his eyes, and hugs me so tightly, it hurts. When will I see him again? I have no idea.

"Take care, okay?" he says, giving me one last squeeze.

"I will," I promise. "I'll call you when I've arrived, all right?"

We are not big on the phrase *I love you* in my family.

But he tries to tell me with his eyes and his hug what he can't say with words. I understand. I love him too.

After he's left, I wander around for a while, trying to regain my composure. And slowly, the sadness I felt over our goodbye is replaced with happy anticipation. Only twelve more hours until I see Richard!

Twelve hours later, we finally touch down in Vancouver. After getting my new red suitcase, I quickly dash into the bathroom to brush my teeth, fix my hair, and put some lip gloss on.

That done, I head to the exit, giddy with excitement.

Where is he?

And then I see him, leaning against a pillar. I start running, and he is walking towards me quickly, with a smile as bright as the sun on his face.

We embrace each other for a long, long time.

"You are here," he finally says.

"Yes, I am," I confirm happily.

"Welcome home."

Chapter 17
A NEW BEGINNING

Richard has rented a two-bedroom apartment for us. It's sparsely furnished, a fact he apologizes for.

"I just moved in two days ago," he explains, and I assure him that it's okay. The few pieces of furniture in the apartment are from friends, either given to him at no cost or for a good price. I'm touched that he has friends that support him through this difficult time.

We are both tired, so we go straight to bed, falling asleep with our arms and legs intertwined, not an inch between us.

The next morning, I discover the deliciousness of cinnamon buns. Richard's friend left a box of four, and I taste one for the first time, instantly falling in love with them. I'm addicted to carbs and sweets, and the combination of sweet cinnamon, rich cream cheese icing, and buttery pastry is heaven on earth.

"Yum, try one," I yell to Richard, who's still in bed. "They are the best thing I've ever tasted!"

"Ughnanwnanrn," is his response. He's not a morning person.

While he's in bed, I explore my surroundings. The apartment is on the ground floor, with the landlord and his family living above us. Upon opening the front door, you step directly into the combined living/dining/kitchen area. Straight ahead is the dining room, with a glass-topped dining table and four upholstered floating dining chairs. This is part of the stuff Richard got from a friend, and while it's not exactly my taste, I'm grateful that we have something to sit on.

To the right is the living room, with a three-seater couch pushed against the wall, a comfortable-looking easy chair and foot stool in brown upholstery, and a brand-new TV set in the corner. As it turns out, the TV is the only thing Richard bought new; typical guy.

The kitchen is plain but functional, with white built-in cupboards and a basic stove, fridge, and dishwasher.

To the left, a narrow hallway leads to the two bedrooms and one bathroom. Our bedroom is furnished with a queen-sized mattress on top of a box spring, and an ancient looking dresser with a gigantic mirror on top.

The other bedroom is completely empty.

When Richard gets up, he tells me that he has to go to his house to feed the animals.

I'm surprised. "Your ex isn't feeding them?"

"No, they're mine."

Mystified, I ask if I can come along.

"Sure."

This is the first time that I see my new neighbourhood by daylight. Our apartment is located right next to a plant nursery, a few minutes out of town. The town itself is small and quaint, if a bit shabby.

On our ten-minute drive to his house we pass small farms, neatly kept residential areas, and a few huge mansions. It all looks foreign to me, so very different from what I'm used to.

Then we pull into the driveway of Richard's place, and I see it for the first time. It's a pretty two-story house with Cedar siding, green shutters, and a big porch, set back from the road in a front yard that looks like a park. There are large cedar and poplar trees in the yard, with a wide expanse of still-green lawn underneath them. A few chickens pick around on the ground, and three dogs come running up to the gate, barking excitedly and wagging their tails. Still sitting in the car, Richard points out where the barn and stables are ("if you walk down the driveway, they are in the back, to the left"), and then he looks at me uncertainly.

I'm suddenly nervous.

"Are they all in the house?" I whisper, and when Richard nods, I shrink into my seat.

"I can't go in there!" I say in a panic. "Can I wait here?"

We decide that it's probably for the best, and then Richard gets out, promising to be back soon.

At this point I'm sitting on the floor in front of the passenger seat, just peeking over the dashboard once in a while to see what's going on outside.

Nothing. Everything is quiet.

I glance up to the large picture window on the first floor, and when I see movement, I duck my head down quickly, terrified that they may have seen me.

I stay on the floor until Richard returns.

Two days later, the next shock: Richard tells me that his two youngest daughters are coming for a visit.

Here's the thing: I'm not a kid-person. Kids scare me. They are unpredictable (once, a little girl poked my breasts and asked, "What are these things good for?"—excellent question, kid), they are brutally honest ("why are your toes so red? They look ugly"—I'm sensitive about my feet, because I know that they are ugly. Thanks for reinforcing my insecurities), they are exhausting.

I have babysat exactly once, and those were the longest two hours of my life. Children sense fear, and the three devils I was responsible for knew that I was terrified of them within the first two minutes. I bribed them with candy they weren't supposed to have, and told them they could do whatever they wanted in the hopes that they would leave me alone. I should have known better.

What they wanted to do was stare at me, inform me regularly that they were bored, and tell me how much more fun they had with all the other babysitters.

After that, I kept a healthy distance from kids. I took comfort in the notion that many parents say they only like their own kids, and after all, I was only twenty-three—I had tons of time to decide on the kid-question.

Except, I don't have tons of time. They are coming later today, and I'm in a panic. What if they hate me? I'm sure they will hate me. Every movie and sitcom featuring kids determined to bring their parents back together pops into my mind, and I'm sure I'm doomed. Not only am I hopeless with children in general, these have a specific reason for disliking me: I'm their dad's new girlfriend.

Obviously, I have known all along that Richard has children.

In the weeks leading up to my move, lonely and eager for my new life,

I concocted an elaborate fantasy: that we will become the perfect patchwork family. The kids will all like me. Since we are close in age (the oldest ones are only eight years younger than me), we will become best of friends. They will share boyfriend troubles with me, we will have raucous and lively family dinners, and they will come to me with all their problems and little secrets.

Their mother will find true happiness with a new guy, and we are all going to live happily ever after.

Joke's on me: I'm a dreamer, not a realist. Knowing that I will have to face real, flesh-and-blood children with active minds and mouths scares the crap out of me.

I try to convince Richard to have them over another day, but no luck. He seems to think that the sooner we do it, the better.

An hour later he leaves to pick them up, and I try to calm myself. How scary can a six-year old and an eleven-year old be? In this moment: extremely scary.

Not only because they are kids, but also for another fact: they only speak English. Richard and I speak German with each other, because my English is basically non-existent.

I'm a wreck. When the door opens, I'm shaking with nerves.

The little one scampers in first. She doesn't look scary; she's tiny, barely three feet tall. She has her father's bright blue eyes, an adorable button nose, and her brunette hair is cut in a stylish bob a la Mia Wallace from Pulp Fiction. At first, she doesn't pay much attention to me, because she's more interested in exploring the apartment. Once she has seen it all, she turns to me.

"Who are you?"

In halting English, I tell her my name and that I'm her dad's friend. She seems satisfied with that.

"I'm Isabella. I have a pony whose name is Pickles, and a white bunny that a man at the auction gave me. Her name is Snowflake. This is my sister Rachel." She points at the other girl, tall and skinny, with hair so blond it's almost white, and pretty green eyes. Rachel greets me with a sweet smile, and then announces that she's hungry.

"I thought we'd go out for dinner?" Richard says, looking at me questioningly.

"You guys go, I stay here," I say, feeling raw and overwhelmed.

Despite his cajoling, I insist that I want to stay home. When they finally leave, I fall onto the couch, and stare up at the ceiling.

Kids. Can I really do this?

To my dismay, they are back fifteen minutes later.

"The girls thought you must be hungry, and asked if we could eat here."

Richard has a look of pride and relief on his face. I gaze at them, at their kind and innocent faces, and catch Rachel's eye. She smiles at me and gestures for me to join them at the table.

Something in me loosens.

Maybe this could work.

Chapter 18

TRUST AND MISTRUST

Over the next few weeks, we establish a routine.

Richard drives to his place twice a day to feed the animals. After the hiding-on-the-floor-of-the-car incident, we both agree that it's more comfortable for all parties involved when I stay home. While he's gone, I watch home-improvement shows on TV to learn English, and pore over the two recipe books my family gave me for Christmas. Not only am I determined to learn English as quickly as possible, I also want to learn how to cook. My current repertory of recipes is limited to three: I can make spaghetti, crepes, and a mean eggnog cake. While I could live off those three meals for weeks, I don't think anybody else could (their loss). Besides, I have noticed that Canada doesn't seem to have eggnog available year-round.

Armed with my thick dictionary, I meticulously translate the ingredients into English, and then we go to the store and buy what I need. Several mishaps happen in the beginning: I answer the question of if I need help finding something with "yes, where can I find floor, please?" (I'm looking for flour, but mispronounce it as 'floor'. You should have seen the clerk's face.)

Another time, the frying pan catches on fire, because I let the oil get too hot.

I don't know that chicken *isn't* done when it's still pink inside, and once I heat up a jar of Sauerkraut in the microwave and wonder why it doesn't taste like my grandma's.

Omelettes are my nemesis, because I always put too much stuff in them, resulting in a pan filled with sausage and vegetables, with some lonely bits of scrambled egg floating in between.

But most of the time, my attempts at cooking pay off. I carefully follow the recipes, and the results are delicious, home-cooked meals.

When I'm not cooking or watching TV, we are horseback riding. It's a mild winter, and part of my fantasy of living in Canada is to become an accomplished horsewoman. Richard has an experienced, gentle old gelding, and he becomes "my" horse. Unbeknownst to me, he simply follows Richard's horse, instead of listening to my questionable commands. I'm under the mistaken assumption that I'm a natural!

Every weekend, Isabella and Rachel come over for a sleepover.

We have pizza- and movie-nights on Fridays, and watch cartoons for hours on Saturday mornings. Isabella is still at that age where she gets up at six in the morning, but she quietly goes to the living room, turns on the TV, and snuggles up on the couch.

I usually join her an hour later, and as soon as I do, Isabella starts doing what she likes best: talk. That girl has boundless energy and charisma, and she proceeds to tell me about everything that goes on in her life: school, pets, her sisters, the TV shows and movies she's into, how annoying that boy Mike is, what food she does and doesn't like at the moment.

A couple of hours later, Rachel will come in. Rachel has got to be the most easygoing girl in the world. She is gentle, patient, and kind, and never seems to get irritated.

Both have gotten used to my terrible English, and correct me whenever I say something wrong, which is often. This turns out to be a blessing, because as I'm learning, nobody else will do it. People are too polite to point out when I use the wrong word or poor grammar, which is well-intended, but not helpful. Kids don't have that false sense of decorum; they simply tell you when something isn't right. I'm grateful for that.

When Richard gets up, we all have breakfast together, and then we do something fun: go for ice cream, the animal auction, for rides with the horses, bowling, or just baking cookies together. The girls love to help me, and I'm so grateful that they like me, I let them do whatever they want.

It's all very easy. Rachel and Isabella seem to have fully accepted the current situation, and things between us are going great.

Unfortunately, that's not how others perceive our relationship.

Richard is having a much more difficult time; his friends think he has lost his mind.

After having tried—and failed—to talk some sense into him, Richard's best friend and his wife have retreated from him. They seem to have taken sides against him. While he is hurt, his commitment to me doesn't change; if anything, it becomes even stronger.

Most of his other buddies' opinions range from "good for him for landing a young chick" (gross) to making bets on how long it will last (the longest we get is six months).

And then there is the guy who has taken an instant dislike to me: Donald. He is convinced that I'm a gold digger and an opportunist, only in it for money and to get a permanent visa for Canada. As much as Richard is in love with me and trusts me, Donald manages to get under his skin. After all, we don't know each other very well—what if he's right?

I saved $3000 before I moved, and that's all my money in the world. Not knowing when I will be able to work (I don't have a work visa), I'm holding on to that money with an iron fist. Richard houses me, feeds me, and generally takes care of me—proof in Donald's mind that I'm using him.

"Why would a young woman want to be with a man who could be her father? There's only one reason: she's after your money. She will milk you dry, and when she has enough of you, she will go back home. Are you sure you want to give up everything for *her*?"

Donald the Meddler manages to plant a seed of doubt in Richard's mind. Even though he trusts me, our relationship is still new and fragile, and we end up having our first fight because of Donald.

Instead of having an honest conversation about his doubts, Richard accuses me of using him.

I'm upset that he doesn't trust me.

"Just because your friend is too narrow-minded to believe that we fell in love with each other doesn't mean it's not true. I thought you knew better. Has it occurred to you that he's probably never experienced anything like we have, and that's why he can't handle it? People don't trust what they don't understand."

At first, we argue, then we talk, and in the end, we make up, Richard apologizing for doubting me.

"It's so hard to listen to them all the time," he confides. "Do you know that nobody gives us a chance?"

I didn't know. Being a stranger here, I don't have to deal with people's opinions and so-called advice. I spend my days with the kids and with

Richard, sheltered from the judgment of others.

I hug him close, and tell him to hell with other people. It's us against the world!

Another time, Richard drives to his old house and doesn't come home. I wait and wait, at first annoyed, then increasingly panicked. I've always had the tendency to get worried when loved ones are out on the road and don't return at the time I expect them, convinced that they have been in a terrible car accident. Once the thought lodges in my mind, I can't shake it off. It stays there, festering, getting me more and more worked up. It's awful.

I don't know what to do. I don't have a phone to call him; I don't know if there is a payphone nearby (as I will learn later, there isn't). I could ask the landlord living above us to use their phone, but I'm too shy.

After three hours of waiting, I'm so hysterical that I decide to walk to the house and check if his truck is there. I don't plan on going in (hell, no!), I just want to make sure that his truck is there and he's still alive.

There's only one small problem: I don't know exactly how to get there. Despite having been a passenger numerous times when Richard drives from the apartment to the house, I haven't been paying that much attention.

No matter. Everything is better than going crazy in the apartment!

I bundle up and set off on foot. It takes twenty minutes to get into town. That part is easy, I've walked it before. But where to next? There are several different routes, but I can't visualize any of them. I randomly select one, and keep walking.

I am so freaked out, tears are streaming down my face. Luckily, it's a Sunday afternoon in January, and nobody else is out and about. When the odd car passes, I turn my face away from the road so they can't see my tears. After what feels like hours, but is probably less than half an hour, a car stops next to me. Oh my God, what if it's a rapist? Nobody knows where I am! If he kills me, they will never find out what happened! I consider jumping into the ditch and climbing up the steep embankment on the other side, trying to escape, when a warm, motherly voice calls out to me, "Can we give you a ride, honey?" I glance towards the car, and see a grey-haired woman in her sixties leaning out of the open passenger side window, smiling at me.

"No, thank you," I call out, hiding as much of my face as possible behind my hair.

"Are you sure?" she asks again, concern in her voice.

"Yes, yes," I nod my head vigorously. "Just walking, ahem, ah." I can't think of the words, so I pump my arms energetically and mimic a power walk. Then it comes to me, "Exercise, exercise!"

"Okay," she says doubtfully, and finally, they drive off.

I feel so conspicuous that I turn on my heel and hurry back home.

I spend the rest of the afternoon imagining the worst.

Richard had an accident and is in the hospital.

Richard is dead.

Richard and his ex reconciled.

Richard's buddies are brainwashing him into leaving me.

By the time he finally comes back, hours later when it's already dark outside, I'm numb with exhaustion. My face is red and blotchy, my eyes tiny, swollen slits.

"I'm sorry I'm so late!" he says upon entering, and then stops abruptly. "What happened?" he asks in alarm.

"Where were you all this time?" I whisper. "I …," I can't find the words to explain what I've been through.

"Some friends were at the house. I completely forgot about it. They don't know yet about the separation, and we didn't want to bring it up today—so I stayed for coffee and dinner. Sorry I didn't tell you, like I said, I had forgotten."

You may recall that we don't have a phone at the apartment, just his cellphone, which he always has with him because of the kids and work. Short of driving back and telling me in person, there was no way for him to let me know about the delay.

Oh, new relationships. Such incredible highs and devastating lows.

The price for all the excitement and fantastic sex is uncertainty, doubt, and jealousy.

I don't know him well enough yet to completely trust him. Everything derisive that has been said about us— "it will never last," "he will get bored of her," "they are too different"—has been scrolling in my head like the ticker tape at the bottom of a TV news channel. My nerves are frayed, my emotions raw.

I'm mad, overwrought—and afraid. Will we survive? Will it ever get easier? Am I strong enough for this?

It was fun in Spain, with no other people around and no need to explain our relationship to anybody. But now, there are so many people with opinions, so many potential traps to fall into. There are family and friends, neighbours and co-workers, parents of the kids' friends who will all find out sooner or later. So much judgment, so little control over it.

Fortunately, Richard has had a strong day. He talks me off the ledge, assures me that yes, it *will* get easier and no, he will never give up on us.

He's had bad days too, where he feels vulnerable and in need of a shoulder to lean on. Believe it or not, I can be that person. There are many days where I'm so happy, I want to dance with joy. Which I do. Badly, but with enthusiasm. On those days, I'm the strong one, full of rose-coloured optimism for our future.

Today, my rose-coloured glasses are nowhere to be found. But that's okay, because Richard has my back. We have each other's.

Spring has arrived, and Richard is back to work. After having been cooped up in the apartment for three days straight without a phone or computer, I'm so bored that I ask if I can come to work with him. Besides, it's dangerous to be left alone with my mind for too long. Someone (usually me) could get hurt.

He agrees, and the next day I put on my oldest jeans and work boots, and tag along.

He is landscaping a new apartment complex in North Vancouver, and the job site is busy. Carpenters, painters, and electricians are tripping all over each other, and they keep messing up our landscape outside. The atmosphere is tense, and it doesn't help that it's raining hard for days on end. We trudge through the mud, getting soaked to the skin every day, no matter how waterproof our rain gear supposedly is. It's miserable, but at least I'm learning two facts about myself: I can rule out landscaping as a possible career, and I'm way less into working outside than I expected. Huh, who knew? My former career choice of becoming a forest ranger was even more ill-advised than I thought.

The other benefit of going to work are the lunches. The guys aren't fans of a packed lunch, and we eat out every day! Such a novelty for provincial little me. My favourite is sushi, which is also entertaining: if we order a big platter to share, you should see us all speed-eating our way through it. You can't trust the next guy to leave the best pieces for you, because he won't. You snooze, you lose, man! Lucky for me, I'm a fast eater, and I can hold my own with the guys. Nobody gets between me and my salmon sashimi!

Also, my English is improving! One of the guys has a beautiful speaking voice, ideal for someone learning a new language: he talks slowly and clearly, enunciating every word perfectly. Once I've overcome my annoying shyness, I talk to him all the time.

With my English teachers being construction workers and two children aged seven and eleven, my vocabulary is interesting.

From the girls, I learn the meaning of wedgies, Wet Willies (in theory and practice), bum drops (when you jump on the trampoline and go butt first), poop piles (manure pile) and mop heads (a breed of chickens that rock a complicated hairdo that looks like an afro).

On the other hand, I overhear (and later look up) what nookies, thongs, hickies, and bootie calls are.

Add to that the make-over shows I sometimes watch, which teach me the names of all the beauty products I don't use—blush, eyelash curler, falsies (that would be false eyelashes, in case you're as confused as I was), highlighter, beauty blender, etc.—it's quite the education.

Chapter 19
MEETING HIS FRIENDS

Six months after my arrival, the separation is finalized, their assets divided, and Richard's ex has bought a house for herself and the kids. We can move back to his old house, a move Richard has been looking forward to, and I have been dreading.

How weird will it be to live in the house that he used to share with his family?

Answer: *Very*. The first thing I notice upon entering the house is the wedding picture of Richard and his ex on the wall. *Ouch*. Well played.

I take it off the wall, open a random drawer, and shove it in as far as it will go. I really want to throw it away, but I don't dare.

I've been inside the house only once before, when they were all out, and I felt so uncomfortable that I left after a couple of minutes. Now I'm taking a closer look at it all. One thing is obvious: we do not share the same taste in home decor.

The walls are a symphony of brown and beige, my two least favourite wall colours. The kitchen is wallpapered in a blue-and-grey swirly design, same as the bathroom.

Most of the furniture is gone, and the few pieces we brought along from the apartment happen to be mostly brown, which makes the house look like a brown cave. I have fantasies of repainting the entire house in brilliant sunset colours: vivid reds, bright oranges, sunny yellows, and soft pinks.

But the next time the kids come over, Rachel runs from room to room, hugging the walls, telling me how much she loves them, and asking me if I'll keep them the way they are. What can I say, other than to promise that, "Yes, of course I will"?

All the non-renovating frees up a lot of time. And too much free time is a dangerous commodity for my overactive mind. I start brooding about my future. I've been in Canada over six months, and I still don't have the faintest idea what I should do with myself. I can't look for a job because I don't have a work visa, and I don't want to tag along with Richard for the rest of my life. Besides, I'm over landscaping.

Instead of fully enjoying the gorgeous summer and living on a farm, I pace restlessly through the house, glaring at the brown and beige walls and wondering what the hell to do next.

Apparently, the next step is introducing me to all of Richard's friends. Being back in his own house, with the separation official and the divorce proceedings underway, has given him a huge boost of confidence. Richard is ready to show me off; I'm not.

So far, I've only met a small circle of people from his life: his co-workers, a few guys from the Legion, where Richard is a member, and one couple from out-of-town, who came to trade chickens with him. They were nice enough, but the wife kept talking very LOUDLY to me, as if my broken English had to do with my lack of hearing and not the fact that it was a new language to me.

I've been in a safe bubble, and getting out of it is scary. Everybody will judge me! This time, it's not just my usual paranoia talking; I know they will. Obviously, I want them to like me, but I'm not good at social interactions at the best of times, and these are hardly the best of times. All of Richard's friends know his ex, and if his best friend is any indication, they will have taken sides. Somehow, I doubt that they will be on mine.

But I know that if I am going to make a life here with him, I will have to meet them eventually, and reluctantly agree to a sushi date with three other couples.

I agonize what to wear. I have lost the twenty extra pounds I put on during my senior year of high school, a fact that thrills me endlessly, but that also means that none of my clothes fit anymore. I'm reluctant to spend money from my dwindling stash, but this occasion calls for a new outfit.

Luckily, I discover Winners, a clothing store offering brand name clothes at discounted prices.

I buy new jeans, several tops, and a white A-line skirt with pink roses printed on it. I decide to wear the skirt with a simple pink top that matches the colour of the roses.

The outfit is sorted—but what will I say? That's a bigger problem. My English is not bad if I'm talking to people I know. But I'm still thinking in German, translating everything I'm about to say in my head first, which makes for awkward delays in conversations.

The process is like this: someone says something to me. I hear it, translate it into German, then form a response in my head in German and translate it into English before I can respond.

Here's an example:

Random guy at the Legion: "What are you doing with an old fart like Richard? Bahahahaha!"

I'm listening, translating, and then, with a ten-second delay, laughing along: "Hahahaha!"

Now I'm trying to figure out what to say—something funny. Hmm, what to say, what to say...The guy looks expectantly at me, and I'm starting to sweat, because by now at least twenty seconds have passed without me saying anything. A twenty-second pause feels like *forever* in a conversation. Try it, I challenge you!

Eventually, the only response I can think of—in German—is, "He didn't come in a younger version." Now I have to translate it, but I don't quite get it right—what I eventually say, close to **half a minute** after random guy made his remark, is, "He wasn't made younger."

Learning a new language is hard.

And now I will have to face his friends. Successful people who are doctors, nurses, accountants, teachers, lawyers. People who are knowledgeable about politics, current events, and history. And here I am, a college-dropout, who can barely make a simple joke, let alone have an intelligent conversation.

Is it any wonder that I'm panicking?

The only bright spot about this dinner is the food—I adore sushi. I decide that the best approach is to say as little as possible and smile a lot.

On the way to the restaurant, I'm incredibly nervous.

"What if I say something stupid?" My biggest worry.

"What if they don't like me?" This is a close second.

"What if I can't understand what they're saying?" The understanding shouldn't be a problem (fingers crossed), but the speaking? That terrifies me.

Richard keeps telling me to relax and just be myself, which is the stupidest advice he could give me. Being myself? As if! I want to appear *much* more sophisticated and confident than I am, thankyouverymuch.

When we arrive after an hour's drive, I don't want to get out of the car.

"Why don't I wait in the car for you? You can bring me some food later. Just tell them that I'm sick or something!"

He won't have it. "Come on, scaredy cat, it will be fine! Let's go!"

I reluctantly follow him, heart pounding, palms wet. Shit! What if I have to shake hands? Touching someone's cold and clammy hand is so gross. I start to frantically wipe my palms on my skirt, trying to get the moisture off. It doesn't work; my hands suddenly possess superhuman powers of sweat production. I can't get them dry!

As it turns out, we can't shake hands. Richard's friends are already there, sitting cross legged on big pillows on the floor, around a long table. It's too difficult to reach them, so we simply wave at the assembled group. One problem is averted, but the next one becomes apparent immediately: how can I sit down gracefully on the floor in a skirt without flashing anyone? I awkwardly sit down, hastily smoothing my skirt over my legs. Only then do I turn to the woman sitting next to me. She is blond and slim, with a long and narrow face. Her hair hangs down loosely, making her face appear even longer. "Hi, I'm Betty," she says, extending her hand. I have no choice but to shake it, inwardly cringing. If she finds my clammy paw off-putting, she doesn't let on. I like her for that.

"I'm Miriam," I say shyly. "Nice to meet you!"

"Likewise!"

I smile at her, not knowing what else to say, and after a moment, she turns to the person sitting on her other side and picks up the conversation they had before our arrival.

I exhale.

Then I glance around at the group of people assembled here. My first impression? They are so *old*! I know from Richard that all his friends are older than him (except for Betty next to me—she's the baby of the group), and they look it. The guys have gray hair, the women wear theirs in practical short styles (again, with Betty being the only exception), and they are dressed in subdued colours.

Sheesh, how will I ever fit in with them?

I try to figure out what they're talking about, but with three separate conversations going on, it's too difficult for me. I give up, and settle in for a long night.

It is long. If you have ever sat in complete silence at a dinner party, you know what it feels like. It's horrendous.

The only thing worse? When the kind man across from me—I think his name is John?— addresses me at some point, asking me something I didn't catch. "I'm sorry?" I ask, turning red.

He asks again, while every other conversation dies down, and all eyes are on me. "How do you like Canada, Miriam?"

Deep breath. This is an easy question! I can do this. I just wish they wouldn't all stare at me.

"I love it," I say. "Everybody is so nice!" And that's it. I can't think of anything else. He looks at me encouragingly, but I've turned mute. After an awkward pause that seems to last an eternity, conversation once again resumes.

I turn to Richard. "Can we please leave soon?" I whisper in desperation. "I can't handle it any longer."

"Okay," he says, giving my hand a reassuring squeeze. It takes him another twenty minutes to get going, and when we're finally outside the restaurant, I have tears in my eyes.

"This was horrible. They must think I'm such a silly girl," I fret, and then I break down in sobs.

"I couldn't think of anything to say! Everybody was staring at me! They must think you made a terrible mistake, choosing me!"

Richard tries to console me, but to no avail. I'm convinced I blew it.

Fortunately, the next meeting with a friend of his goes a lot better. Once again, we go to a sushi restaurant, but this one is more casual and has proper tables and chairs.

I've heard a lot about this friend: he's Australian, a wicked good cook, always up for an adventure, with a fondness for good food and drink.

We meet him outside the restaurant. The guys embrace each other in a man hug, and once they let go, Richard makes the introductions. "Miriam, this is Owen. Owen, meet my girl, Miriam."

"It's a pleasure to meet you, Miriam," Owen says in his awesome Aussie accent, and gives me a hug. Then he turns to Richard and says, "How did you old dog land such a beauty?" Oh, what a charmer—I like him immediately.

This meal couldn't be more different from the last one. The boys talk and laugh, and while I'm still more listening than speaking, I laugh along with them and have a great time. Owen makes an effort to include me into the conversation, and asks me lots of questions about Germany and myself. He is generous with his compliments, repeatedly telling me how good my English is. This is probably a lie, but it works; I'm so at ease, I speak much more freely than I usually do with strangers.

When we say goodbye, I know I have made a new friend. We promise to meet again soon, and I float home on clouds.

And then I meet *the lawyers*.

Before I take you along to the first eye-opening party, here's a disclaimer: all names and places have been changed. (That goes for everyone in this book, but I thought it prudent to repeat this important fact.) No need to sue my ass!

Okay, with the legalities out of the way, here's the backstory to *the lawyers*.

When Richard first met them, none of them were lawyers yet. They were hard-partying, fun-chasing college students, and they hit it off right away. Richard may not have been a college student, but he could party hard and chase fun with the best of them. Fast forward twenty-five years, and they are now fear-inducing attorneys with respectable careers; but their old ways are still there, hiding under a glossy surface.

I don't know what they will think of us, but being lawyers, divorces are hardly a novelty to them. I expect they have seen much more scandalous relationships than ours.

As always, Richard is useless in predicting how they might react to me, and once again I have to go in blind, hoping for the best. As you can probably guess, I'm nervous. *Again.* Honestly, this new life gig is exhausting!

We're headed towards the ritzy part of town. The houses get bigger the further we drive along, with manicured front lawns, tall gates, tennis courts, and swimming pools everywhere you look.

I didn't grow up hobnobbing with rich people; my parents are firmly middle-class, and so are all their neighbours and friends. My mother has such respect for people she regards as above her in status that it borders on fear, and I have no reason to believe that she is wrong. Will they look down on me?

Well, I'm about to find out, because we have arrived.

The house is massive: snow-white pillars flank the imposing entrance, the door is 10-feet tall, and through the windows I see a giant chandelier hanging in the vestibule lit up with hundreds of lights. The sound of music and laughter is floating out, mixed with the delicious smell of roasting meat.

The door flies open, and a small woman stands there, brilliantly illuminated in the light spilling out behind her, wine glass in hand, smiling broadly.

"Richard! Welcome! Fashionably late as always, but I'm glad you made it. Come in, come in!" She laughs and embraces him, standing on her tiptoes. She's barely five feet tall, but her personality makes more than up for it. She seems larger than life!

Behind her, two men appear, matching smiles on their handsome faces. One of them is huge, at least six feet three inches, 280 pounds, but with a beautiful, gentle smile. The other one is shorter, incredibly buff, with short-cropped hair, gleaming white teeth, and a wicked twinkle in his eyes. They look thrilled to see Richard, and there's much back-slapping and bro-hugging happening for a while. Then, everybody's attention focuses on me.

"Guys, this is Miriam," Richard introduces me—and then, after a short pause, "my girlfriend."

It's the first time he has introduced me as such! All the times before, he would simply say my name, leaving it up to the other person to figure out who exactly I was to him.

Three pairs of green eyes take me in—two pairs approvingly, the other one questioningly.

"Miriam, sweetheart, you are a sight for sore eyes," the large man says warmly, enveloping me in his big arms. "It's so nice to meet you. I'm Cooper."

The other one steps forward, his eyes twinkling merrily. "Richard doesn't deserve you!" he calls, looking me up and down in an exaggerated fashion and whistling through his teeth. "Rich, you lucky bastard, hold on to her before she comes to her senses!" He also goes in for a hug, whispering in my ear, "Don't look so scared, baby girl. You gonna be fine." In his normal voice, he introduces himself as Jerome, Cooper's younger brother.

The last one to greet me is the small woman. She is gracious, but more reserved than the guys.

"I'm Amelia. Make yourself at home! Can I get you a drink?"

As it turns out, she is the older sister to the guys, and this is her house.

We follow her into the kitchen, where the party is in full swing. She pours me a glass of wine and gestures to the bar for Richard to help himself. Then she excuses herself to look after her other guests, and I get a chance to look around.

We are standing in a large, luxurious kitchen. Everything is state of the art: the appliances are industrial-sized and shiny, the countertops are marble, and the glass I'm drinking from looks like it's crystal. There are about twenty guests milling about, in various shapes and ethnicities, but they all have one thing in common: they look polished. Expensive haircuts, even more expensive clothes, and gold- and diamond-jewellery dripping from most necks, ears, arms, and fingers. Oh-my-god. What are *we* doing here? Out of the corner of my eye I see Richard walking past me purposefully, clearly with a destination in mind. I clamp on to him like a koala to a tree, determined not to let go of him. I won't be stranded by myself at this party, nuh-uh!

We are headed to a group of people gathered around Jerome, who's keeping the assembled group in stitches. As he sees us approach, he seamlessly switches to an Arnold Schwarzenegger accent. "Look whosse choining uss nouw, itss Remmington Richaad und de luyvely frollein Miyium. Come on, come on, haff a drink wid uss! Sit offuh deyah."

What the hell? Amused, I sit down as indicated.

"Why 'Remington Richard'?" I can't help but ask, forgetting that I'm supposed to be intimidated by these people.

"Luyvely Miyium, datss a greid story, chust greid," Jerome twinkles at me, and I laugh. His Arnie interpretation is just too funny!

He immediately recounts the tale of a party that happened many years ago, where the boys, after hours of drinking, had the brilliant idea to do some light target shooting in the backyard. At 1 a.m. In the middle of the city. The only one who had a rifle handy was none other than Remington Richard, which is how he acquired the name. The target practice was cut short by the arrival of the cops, but by sheer luck (and an impressive display of quick thinking, considering the circumstances), Richard managed to throw the rifle over the fence into the neighbour's yard. They all feigned innocence, helpfully pointing out that there were no weapons here, and that the shots that were heard must have come from somewhere else. The police were suspicious, but without the proverbial smoking gun, they couldn't do anything. They told the party revelers to keep the noise down, and left.

More people have joined our circle, and a beautiful man with a neatly trimmed beard, chocolate skin, and half a dozen diamond rings on his fingers sits down beside me.

He introduces himself as Leroy, and then says, "I'm so glad you are here tonight. You are the only other person under the age of 40! Being the youngest amongst these old geezers was getting boring." He continues, "I know you're not supposed to ask that, but how old are you, pretty girl?"

"Twenty-three," I answer truthfully.

"Aaahhh, so scandalous!" he squeals excitedly. "I love it! How old is Richard?"

"He just turned 49."

He conspiratorially leans in closer and asks me, "How is the sex?"

"Leroy!" I cry in mock outrage, and swat him away. I want to say something along the lines of, "A lady never kisses and tells," but not having the required language skills, I blush and don't say anything.

Leroy laughs good-naturedly, and then proceeds to tell me that he is 31, his partner is fifteen years older, and that he is addicted to reality TV. We both share an obsession with Tyra Banks' hit show *America's Next Top Model*, and happily discuss the crazy antics of the contestants.

The hours fly by. What strikes me as astonishing is that nobody asks me what I do for a living. In Germany, that's usually the first question someone you meet asks you, presumably to file you into the correct pigeon hole.

Here, nobody does that. They don't seem to care one bit what anybody does for work. They take you at face value, and the common goal for the night is to have fun and enjoy yourselves.

From Richard, I know that many of the party guests are lawyers, others work in finance (whatever that means), some run their own businesses, and one is a model. She is the first model I have seen in real life, and she is breathtaking. At over six feet tall, she has long legs that won't quit, close-cropped hair that highlights her razor-sharp cheekbones, and an overall striking beauty that is intimidating. She is not pretty, but devastatingly gorgeous, and has a regal bearing like a queen.

But for an odd reason, I don't feel out of place. I'm having the time of my life, despite my less-than-perfect English, having no job, no education, and not a single diamond on my person. We're all just having fun, and I feel included.

It's nice—and confusing. All my life, I have been taught to stick to "my kind." Not so much with words, but with actions. I have watched my mom get flustered and nervous when the retired town doctor comes into the store. I have listened to them talk about "the higher ups"—teachers, doctors, lawyers, business men. Everybody who has gone to university is above us.

Subconsciously, I have learnt that the safest way to live is to stay within your own class.

But somehow, I have ended up here, in this gorgeous, expensive home, with people who have impeccable taste, successful careers—and are just as goofy and ridiculous as my college friends. If I wouldn't know anything about them, I wouldn't peg them as "higher class"—I would think they are—well, what, exactly?

They clearly look expensive. They are worldly. But they aren't anything like I always assumed rich people would be. They don't sit around smoking cigars and swigging brandy out of large glasses, philosophising about the state of the world. Instead, they watch reality TV, tell dirty jokes, do an impressive Arnold Schwarzenegger-impersonation, get drunk, and hang out with a landscaper and his inappropriately young girlfriend.

I feel more at home at this party than I have amongst my family or age-appropriate friends. It's unsettling—and incredibly liberating.

I have followed the rules all my life, and where did it leave me? Heartbroken, lost and confused.

If breaking the rules is this exciting, this *dazzling*, why doesn't everybody do it?

Chapter 20

BACK TO SCHOOL

We spend the rest of the year trying to find our new routine. Once school starts, it's established that it makes the most sense if I pick up Rachel and Isabella from school, since I'm the only one in the family who doesn't work.

It's fine. It's the only logical solution to our situation. And I love the girls, so what's the big deal?

And yet.

I'm feeling constricted by this arrangement. As soon as I get up in the morning, I feel stressed.

I constantly watch the time, afraid I may be late in picking them up.

Then there's the daily struggle with figuring out what to make them for lunch. And for dinner.

I quickly realize that I don't mind cooking if I only have to do it once in a while. But doing it every single day, multiple times a day? That's getting old fast. I'm the girl who used to have cereal for dinner at least five nights a week, and now, just a few months later, I'm suddenly a caretaker/nanny/stepmom? who's responsible for two children. It's overwhelming.

But the worst part? The pick-up routine. It takes me exactly one pick-up to understand that there is a strict hierarchy at play under the seemingly innocent mom-jeans and forgiving-sweaters-façade—and I'm at the very bottom.

My first mistake? I arrive ten minutes before the end of school, which means I have to park a couple of blocks away, because the side streets surrounding the elementary school are jam-packed with cars. Little did I know that you have to show up half an hour before school is out if you want one of the prime spots right in front of it. I walk the two blocks to the school—and then I'm at a loss. Where should I wait for the kids? There are clusters of waiting mothers everywhere. They are clutching their travel mugs (some of them containing something a little stronger than coffee, if the rumours are true), animatedly talking to each other, vigorously waving their arms around to emphasize whatever it is they are saying. I feel conspicuous standing alone, and I inwardly berate myself for not having agreed on a specific spot to meet the kids.

Too uncomfortable to stand around, I decide to head inside the school and try to find them there. It's no better inside. There are more mothers, giving me curious once-overs as I enter the building, and I have to suppress the urge to hide in the bathroom. Instead, I slowly walk down the hallway, pretending to look at the displayed artwork. I try to recall the names of the girls' teachers, to pick them up from their class rooms. I can't. Damn it, Isabella must have mentioned her teacher's name at least a hundred times, why can't I remember? I'm the worst caretaker/nanny/stepmother? ever.

Suddenly, the bell rings, the doors open, and a flood of students stampedes down the hallway. I press myself flat against the wall to avoid being run over. I follow the kids outside, craning my neck in the hopes of finding Isabella and Rachel. Gosh, there are a lot of little girls that look like them! Several times I think I spotted one or the other and start towards them, only to realize that I got the wrong child.

By now I'm standing outside again, and I awkwardly lean against the monkey bars, in full view of the waiting vehicles filled with hostile mothers. My back is turned towards them since I'm facing the school, but I imagine them whispering about me, "Who is she? The nanny?"

"No, I hear that's the mistress of Rachel and Isabella's father!"

"What?! No! I can't believe she dares to show her face here. Does she have no shame?"

"Those poor children. It's a disgrace!"

"She's obviously after his money."

"Oh, for sure. Why else would she go after an older man?"

"How old do you think she is? She barely looks legal!"

Do they really say these things? I have no idea. But I swear I feel their eyes bore into my back. If looks could kill, I doubt that I would still be standing here.

After what feels like ten eternities put together, I finally spot Isabella and Rachel in the crowd and rush towards them. I've never been more relieved to see them.

Apart from looking after the girls several days a week, I'm also in charge of the horses. Again, it makes the most sense for me to clean the stable, since I'm the one with all the time in the world. But mucking stalls, trudging through pouring rain and pushing a heavy wheelbarrow through ankle-deep mud is as much fun as it sounds, and gives me way too much time to think.

And increasingly, what I think is this: what am I doing? I'm almost twenty-four, and I still don't have any idea what I should do with my life. I may be in a relationship and in Canada now, but in many ways, I'm no further ahead than I was a year ago. Am I supposed to work on a farm and look after two kids whom I love, but who aren't mine, for the rest of my life?

I love Richard. But once again I'm living the life of the guy I'm with, instead of figuring out what *I* want.

The days pass slowly, with me mucking and brooding, cooking and keeping house. The evenings are much more fun, because then Richard is home and we get to spend time together. I'm happy with him, but unhappy with the rest of my life. I *have* to do something.

By now it's November, and I have been in Canada for ten months. My English has become decent, and I'm dying to earn money. However, I still don't have a work permit, so I decide to look for a school I could go to.

The next few pages are a cautionary tale about how not to decide on a career path. As you may have gathered from my misguided Forestry-experience, I don't have the best track record when it comes to choosing a career.

My next career choice is much worse.

Buckle your seat belts, and take notes of what *not* to do!

I rack my brain for what in the world I might be interested in. Nothing that takes years and years—I'm still not in the mood for continuing education, but feel that I don't have a choice at this point.

Mistake number one: If you don't know what you want, don't go to school for something random. It didn't work the first time, remember?

Aside from the criteria that it's quick, I also want it to be easy. So, medicine is out. Ha, joking! I'm way too dumb for anything related to medicine. I briefly consider something that's related to writing/journalism/books, but dismiss the idea almost immediately. I can't properly speak the language, how in the world could I manage to write it? Ridiculous.

Mistakes number two-five: Not identifying your interests correctly. Underrating the importance and magic power of hard work. Underestimating your abilities. Negative self-talk. Not knowing your strengths and weaknesses.

Phew, that's a lot! And we're just getting started.

As I'm morosely surfing the World Wide Web in search of inspiration, I come across an advertisement. Sounds familiar, doesn't it? All my big decisions seem to be preceded by an online ad. Anyway, this one is from The Canadian Tourism & Hospitality College. They offer certificate and diploma programs in hospitality, and with great interest I learn that the certificate-course only takes six months. They claim that they guarantee a job placement, and when I see that the closest campus is located only half an hour away from my house, my excitement rises.

I fondly remember our road trip through Spain the previous year, and how much I enjoyed my stays in various hotels. How bad could it be to work in one?

I immediately start to imagine myself in a smart suit, perfectly coiffed hair and make-up, being part of a close-knit staff that feels like family. Oh, in case I haven't mentioned it yet, despite the kids and Richard's friends, I feel quite lonely a lot of the time. Making up an imaginary work family gives me so much pleasure, that I'm ready to start work right now. Where can I sign up?

Mistake number six: Base your decision on unrealistic expectations and an epic, sex-crazed vacation that was as far removed from reality as it possibly gets.

That evening, I excitedly tell Richard about it. His reaction is much more reserved than what I think is appropriate, but since this is the first time I have mentioned wanting to work in hospitality, it's probably not surprising. However, I convince him to go to the college with me and check it out. The next day I email them to enquire further, and in the ensuing correspondence we make an appointment to visit them the following week.

Mistake number seven: To not think carefully about it, but to jump right in. Also, doing as little research as possible beforehand. You have never heard of The Canadian Tourism & Hospitality College? Who cares? It has 'college' right in its name, so it must be a college.

When we arrive at the address they gave me, I'm taken aback. There's a dusty little music store where I expect the grand college to stand. Did I get it wrong? I check the street name and number, and it's the one they gave me. Hesitantly, I go inside the store and approach the bearded, bored-looking guy behind the counter.

"Uhm, excuse me," I start, "I'm looking for the tourism college?" He points a thumb up to the ceiling, not bothering to make eye contact. "First floor," he says, continuing to stare at his computer screen. I thank him and go back to the car where Richard is waiting, to let him know that we are, indeed, in the right place. As I look up the building, I see a poster-sized sign propped up in a window on the first floor, with "The Canadian Tourism & Hospitality College" written on it. Huh. Quite different from my previous school, but I tell myself that this might be perfectly normal here. "Keep an open mind," I encourage myself, and we enter the building.

Mistake number eight: Ignoring your gut feeling.

We take the elevator and exit onto a dark, dingy floor with dirty-looking carpet. A sheet of paper with the school logo and an arrow points us into the right direction.

There are several doors leading into what I later learn are offices, and then we stand in front of the "college." I knock, and when I don't hear anything, I push open the door carefully. We step into a little office with a desk, a water cooler, and three open doors leading into further rooms. One is a classroom, one is the staffroom, and the third is the director's office. That's it.

A blond, carefully made-up woman in her forties approaches us with a wide smile.

"Hello, you must be Miriam. Welcome! I'm Monique, the director."

I shake her outstretched hand and introduce Richard.

She beckons us into her office and begins her spiel. She tells us about the ever-growing hospitality industry and the limitless opportunities it affords to young people starting their career. When I mention that I'm nearly twenty-four, she laughs gaily and assures me, "You are a baby; you have your entire life ahead of you!"

She paints a glittering picture of traveling the world, being able to work anywhere I want, of flexible hours, fun and adventure. I nod along and smile, not getting a word in, but Richard sits next to me with a stony face, looking at Monique steadily. I know him well enough by now to recognize that he doesn't trust her. She must sense it too, because she gets increasingly more flustered. Her smooth delivery gets choppy; she stumbles over words, loses her train of thought, and at one point she seems to be at a loss for words.

Feeling sorry for her, I interrupt the awkward silence with a few questions of my own.

Is my English adequate for attending school? Oh yes, it's excellent, naturally.

We go over class times (every day from two to six o'clock in the afternoon), exam schedules, and job opportunities.

And then, I address the elephant in the room, since nobody else is bringing it up: how much will it cost? I've tried to find the information on their website, but it wasn't on it. I also asked in one of my emails, but they were evasive and insisted to tell me in person.

Monique doesn't come right out with the number either. Instead, she seems to be gearing up to repeat the highlights of her speech to emphasize everything I will be getting by attending her school.

For the first time during the entire meeting, Richard speaks up. "Cut to the chase. How much?"

Monique looks startled, but doesn't dare to disobey. In a slightly quivering voice, she says, "$8,000.00."

I'm dismayed. Eight thousand dollars? That seems a lot of money for a one-semester course. I tell her I'll think about it, and we leave.

On the way home, I press Richard for his opinion, but he insists that I have to decide on my own if I want to do it or not.

Mistake number nine: Closing your eyes tightly so you won't have to look at the red, flashing warning lights that you know are there. Ignoring your common sense, instinct, and your much more life-experienced partner's gut feeling.

Any normal person would listen to the warning bells going off in her head, but I don't. Because once again, I don't know what else to do, and it seems better to do something that's probably a mistake, instead of doing some serious soul searching. I don't want to look at myself too closely, afraid of what I might find.

Mistake number ten: Not doing any soul searching out of fear. Silly, silly girl.

The immediate problem is the tuition; I don't have it. Who can I ask for the money? Pride and shame won't permit me to ask my parents for it. Richard? He hasn't offered, but I know that he will lend it to me if I ask. But I know that he thinks the school is shady (I secretly agree with him, but won't admit it), even though he hasn't said a single word, and I hesitate to ask for his help.

Help comes from a source I didn't even consider: my grandmother. Before her retirement, she worked in a factory, and her pension isn't much, so I would never have asked her. But I mention my plans of going to school when I call her, and she insists on giving me the money. She bought my sister Emma a new kitchen as a wedding present, and since it's unclear if I will ever get married, Oma wants to do this for me.

I'm touched. I swear to myself that I will work my ass off to make her generous gift worthwhile, and in January 2004, I start my hospitality program.

There are five students in my class: Wei-Ping from Hong Kong, three girls from around here, and me. Our teacher is a motherly, sweet woman who has five kids, took an online teaching program, and who is now teaching for the very first time. It becomes clear from the first day that I am the star student. Wei-Ping only speaks when asked a direct question, and even then, it's never more than a couple of words.

Nicole, one of the girls, is increasingly distracted by problems at home, and drops out halfway through.

Taryn, the second girl, is nice and personable, but lazy; she never does any of the required reading or her homework.

The third girl, Dani, struggles with the course. She gets poor marks in exams, freezes during presentations, and when asked a question, usually gets the answer wrong.

I only speak up on my first day because I feel sorry for Sharon, our nice teacher; she's trying to get us to talk, but none of my fellow students says a word. To break the awkward silence, I answer every question she asks us, a pattern that I will keep up until the last day.

While Forestry school was hard, this one is easy. I can't help but feel proud when Sharon praises me or I get 100% on a test. I'm the best student in the class! I learn to do presentations! And all that in a foreign language! I could be in danger of becoming a self-important asshole, if things at home wouldn't begin to deteriorate.

It's all because of the divorce. In March, Richard's divorce is finalized, and he becomes a bachelor once again for the first time in nineteen years. He's thrilled, and so am I, because now *we* can get married! At least that's my plan. Richard has other ideas. He's just lost half of everything, while he gained a hefty mortgage and monthly child support. Understandably, he is in no hurry to enter round two of the marriage game.

I have never been desperate to get married, but now that he doesn't want to, I'm becoming obsessed. I can't stop talking about it, and we fight more and more.

A word of advice, ladies: nothing puts a guy less in the mood to propose than a nagging girlfriend. Somebody should have told me that, but maybe they did, and I just didn't listen.

In my defense, I have a reason for my urgency to get married: I want to get my permanent resident status for Canada. So far, I bounced from visitor to visitor visa, and currently I have a student visa. But it only lasts until I'm done with school, and what will I do then? I can't think of another way to become a permanent resident than to get married.

Frustratingly, Richard refuses to talk about it. All he'll say is that I'm overreacting and that it will sort itself out.

A word of advice, guys: nothing gets a woman more worked up than being told that she is overreacting. Remember how it feels when you're constantly being nagged about marriage? Yes, it's *that* feeling.

With our relationship going through a rough patch, I focus all my energy on school and the question of what's next. Graduation is in July, and we have started to talk about job opportunities. The school has affiliations with a five-star resort in Wales, and they tell us that we can get a job there if we want to. My German passport enables me to work and live anywhere in The European Union, and if I decide to go for it, I would be earning money again for the first time in a year and a half. I miss having my own money and being independent, and I'm unsure of where Richard and I are headed. If he's so unconcerned about an issue that directly affects our relationship, maybe he's just not that into me anymore?

After agonizing over the problem for weeks, I finally make up my mind: I ask my teachers to sign me up.

They contact the resort, and in June I receive an email that includes a job offer, the promise of paid-for accommodation, and a start date: September 1st.

I guess I'm going to Wales.

Chapter 21

THE END?

I don't tell Richard about my plans. Instinctively, I know that he would talk me out of it, but I doubt that things would change. Deep inside, I have a strong sense that this is what I'm supposed to be doing.

When I'm at home, I force myself not to think about it. I pretend that everything is normal, and I'm doing such a great job pretending that there are stretches of time where I forget that I'm leaving soon. I told him that I want to visit my family and booked a ticket to Germany, something he does regularly, so he doesn't suspect that anything is amiss.

His 50th birthday is on the horizon, and we decide to go away for a romantic weekend to celebrate. We book two nights at a luxury resort at the shores of a picturesque lake, find someone to take care of the farm for the weekend, and we are off.

The weekend is horrible. Not because we are fighting or having a terrible time, but because it's just the opposite: it's lovely. More than lovely, it's like reliving our epic road trip through Spain again. We may have our challenges in normal life, but we are *great* at vacation. We met on vacation, and fell in love on vacation, so vacation is our love language. Richard is always a relaxed guy, but I'm pretty high-strung. Worrying is the name of my game, and I find it impossible to turn off my brain. The voices in my head that tell me how serious life is are always active, whispering their dire warnings, inflicting doubt, making me question my choices. But take me away from my daily routine and put me on the road, in a hotel, or into someone else's house, and I'm a new person. I'm free, because the voices don't seem to like to travel.

The magic of vacation is in full force this weekend. The resort we are staying at is a Canadian classic, built in the 19th century. There are five natural mineral hot springs that are feeding their pools, and the water is said to have healing powers. It smells a bit funky, but feels heavenly, and we frolic in the different pools for hours. Before dinner, we take a stroll alongside the lake, hand in hand. Looking at the beautiful scenery, with the mountains rising majestically behind the lake, my heart is hurting. Am I really going to leave this gorgeous country soon? And the man, who, at this moment, is squeezing my hand, and pulling me in for a hug and a whispered "I love you"? I can barely stand it.

I hug him back, tears in my eyes. When he notices them, he asks softly, "What's wrong? Why are you crying?"

I wipe my eyes hastily, and try to reassure him. "Because I'm happy. It's so romantic! I love you." And I do. Am I really doing the right thing?

We booked a table at their fancy restaurant, a place with a dress code, live band, and famously delicious food. Once we return to our room I have a shower and start to get gussied up. Richard stretches out on the bed to watch some TV, confident that he will be ready in ten minutes.

I choose my outfit carefully: a colorful pencil skirt with tropical flowers, a yellow button-down shirt tucked in to emphasize my butt, heels, and statement earrings. My hair is extremely short, and earrings have become my safety blanket that makes me feel feminine. That, and wearing skirts and dresses.

I put on some make-up, and then I step out into the room to await Richard's reaction.

"What do you think?" I do a little twirl, and Richard whistles approvingly.

"You look hot!" he tells me, and then he gets up to have his shower. He's not into suits, so he wears black jeans, cowboy boots, a crisp white shirt, and his black leather vest. His signature black cowboy hat completes the ensemble, and he looks more handsome than ever.

I feel like a princess when I walk into the elegant restaurant on his arm.

The evening is wonderful. We start with champagne, to toast his birthday. I choose the crab cakes for starters, duck breast for main, and a slice of ginger cake for dessert. Richard has the seared scallops, prime rib, and crème brûlée, his favorite. We share a bottle of wine, and then order a second one. We talk and laugh and have a wonderful time, and as I'm looking into his bright blue eyes, pleasantly tipsy, I catch myself thinking: I don't have to go. I can just stay here! Screw Wales. I don't want to leave him!

We dance, and then stumble to bed, where we make love before falling asleep, tightly intertwined.

I wake up the next morning with a physical and emotional hangover. While Richard is snoring peacefully next to me, I keep thinking about leaving in ten days. I have no idea if I'm leaving him for good, or if it's a temporary thing, since we haven't talked about it. We haven't talked about it because he has no idea about my plans! I'm racked with guilt, but still—for the thousandth time I replay my options, and I see no future here for me without getting a permanent resident visa. But how? That's the problem I can't figure out. Richard refuses to talk about it, so what am I supposed to do? Not for the first time, I wish we could go away on a never-ending road trip, just the two of us, and leave reality behind.

I sigh, and then I get up. I pull the curtain aside and see that it's raining outside. It's just past eight o'clock, and I know that Richard won't get up for at least another hour. I decide to explore the hotel a bit more, and after getting dressed and leaving him a note explaining where I am, I quietly leave the room.

I slowly walk along the long, carpeted corridor, nodding and smiling at the few employees that bustle by. Soon, I will be one of them!

Not at this hotel, but at *the* luxury golf resort in Wales. The position they offered me is 'Food and Beverage Associate at the Convention Centre', which is a long and fancy title for being a waitress for businessmen. The pay is £4.50, about CAN$10.00, which is minimum wage. I try not to think about the fact that I just paid more on tuition per month than what I will be making. What's done is done, and at least I got a job out of it.

I wander around for half an hour, poking my head into the dining room where a few guests are having breakfast, peeking into the gym (deserted), and strolling through the lobby, past the spa, and under the covered walkway between the picturesque pools.

Then I return to our room, where Richard is awake and watching TV.

We spend the day eating, swimming, and checking out the cute little village. The rain stops at lunchtime, and another glorious day unfolds. For dinner, we go to a local restaurant that's overlooking the lake, sitting on their patio and enjoying the sunset. It's been another beautiful day, but I can't wait to go home—it's just too hard.

The next ten days fly by. I go through all my things, trying to decide what to pack. Richard thinks I'm coming back after two weeks, but the truth is, I may never return. I have resolved to take only one suitcase, to avoid rousing suspicion. It's easier than you may think, because I arrived with only one suitcase eighteen months earlier, and I've bought precious little during my time in Canada.

There is still one problem: the hotel is supposed to send my contract by mail. I'm checking the mailbox every day, getting more worried with each passing day when it hasn't arrived yet. What am I going to do if it doesn't make it in time? Will Richard send it to me?

I don't know, so I keep fretting.

Then the day of my departure dawns. I haven't slept all night, because I'm sad beyond words. I stole outside in the middle of the night to cuddle the dogs and cry silent tears before going back to bed, staring wide-eyed at the ceiling, unable to fall asleep.

The contract still hasn't arrived. We have to leave at noon, and usually the mailman doesn't come until two or three o'clock in the afternoon.

The bags are in the car, and we are about to head out, when I nip out to the mailbox one last time, just in case. Low and behold, there it is: a large, fat envelope with UK stamps, wedged inside the mailbox. I can't believe it. If this isn't a clear sign from the universe that I'm doing what I'm supposed to be doing, then I don't know what is. I briefly close my eyes, say a silent *thank you*, and then dash across the street back to the car, stuffing the envelope into my bag before Richard sees it.

Once at the airport, I insist that he let me out in front of the building, instead of coming inside. He hesitates, but I can be persuasive if I want to be, and in the end, he gives in. He helps me with my suitcase, and then I give him a kiss and a fierce hug, before turning and quickly heading inside the terminal. From behind the glass door, I watch him drive away, and tears fill my eyes. Will I ever see him again?

With great difficulty, I pull myself together. It's no use to look back and worry about what could have been; it's time to look ahead. I will spend a month in Germany with my family before going to Wales. My parents know about my plans, and support them wholeheartedly. I can't help but notice the underlying "I told you so" attitude from them, but they are nice enough to not say it out loud.

I'm back at my parent's house for only two hours when the phone rings. Even without caller ID, I know who it is.

"Hello?"

"Are you coming back?"

None of us has announced our names; it's not necessary.

"I don't know."

"I've looked around the house, and I noticed that most of your stuff is gone. Have you left me?"

I hesitate. "I've accepted a job in Wales, starting next month. I don't want to leave you, but I feel like you left me no choice."

[Ominous pause]

Then: "WHAT???!!??"

It appears that he's genuinely surprised. That surprises me.

"Well, YEAH. I've tried to talk to you about my legal status in Canada for *months*. You always blew me off. It didn't seem to be very important to you, but it's important to me! As a matter of fact, my legal status expired yesterday, which is why I left."

Silence.

Me: "Hello? Are you still there?"

Him: "*That's* why you left?"

He seems flabbergasted.

Me: "Yes! I need to be independent! To make my own money! I've told you that for months!"

I actually pull the receiver away from my ear, to look at it. Is this a prank? We've talked about it *all the time*, haven't we?

Apparently not. In, what to me is the *most* severe case of miscommunication *ever*, it slowly emerges that all my 'nagging' and 'going on about it' didn't drive the issue home. *At all.*

I'm slightly worried about his mental well-being at this point.

"You really didn't know? I mean, *not at all??*"

I can't believe it. Richard claims that he's blindsided by my move.

"I know we have had a few problems lately, but we're happy, aren't we?" he asks me pleadingly.

"Well," I start, and then pause, unsure how to explain exactly how I feel. It doesn't help that my parents are in the same room, listening openly. "Hang on a minute," I tell Richard, and then ask my parents if they could please give me same privacy. Damn those phones attached to cords! They get up, my mom with obvious reluctance, and retreat into the living room. I close the door, and return to my conversation.

"You are the most important person to me," I begin. "Meeting you and being with you have been the highlights of my life." Just thinking about him, how we met, everything we have been through, makes me want to cry. I take a deep breath, and continue. "But I don't know if we have a future together. We need to find a way for me to be in Canada, and you don't seem to care about that. I know that you don't want to pay for me for the rest of your life, and I don't want that either! Just the opposite, I hate being financially dependent on you. On anyone. I want to be independent, to be able to stand on my own two feet. No handouts. But to get there, we have to figure out a way, and you refuse to do that. What choice did I have?"

I'm waiting for an answer, but none is forthcoming.

"Are you still there?" I ask quietly.

"Yes, just taking it all in." He pauses. "I really had no idea how important this is to you." I almost roll my eyes when I hear him say that. Men! How dense can they be? Apparently denser than I thought.

In the end, he tells me that he has to see me, and that he's coming to Germany so we can talk about everything in person. I agree, and hang up.

Three days later I'm about to head out the door for a hair appointment, when the phone rings.

"Miriam Meier!"

"I'm driving towards an orange church tower, down a winding, narrow road..."

I'm speechless for a moment. He's describing our local church, two minutes away from us. Then I find my voice. "What?!? Are you *here*? Already??"

"Yes," he confirms, sounding equally excited and hesitant. "I thought I'd surprise you!"

It's a surprise, all right. We only talked a couple of days ago; how did he manage to get to Germany this quickly? He needed to find someone to take care of the farm, book a flight, get here, and then drive the seven hours from his parent's place to mine. My mind is spinning. How did he do all that in 72 hours?

He interrupts my thoughts. "Where do you live?" Oh yeah, he has never been here.

I give him directions, but then add hastily, "I won't be here when you arrive because I have a hair appointment. You will have to talk to my mom until I'm back."

I quickly tell my startled mom that Richard will be here any minute, and then I flee.

When I'm settled in the chair at the hairdresser, I can't believe I just left him with my mother. It was a panic decision, made because he caught me off guard. Now I regret it. What will she tell him? I doubt that she's welcoming him with open arms. My parents hope that I left him for good, and that I will start my life fresh in Wales. No doubt they want a more age-appropriate, uncomplicated relationship for me. I've tried to explain that nothing is decided yet, but listening has never been a strong suit of my mother, who is sure I finally snapped out of my temporary insanity and have come to my senses.

I fidget and fret, and tell the hairdresser not to bother with colouring my hair as we originally planned. I can't wait to get home and do some damage-control. If it's not too late, I think darkly.

Twenty minutes later I'm back at home, where my mom and Richard sit on opposite sides of the table, looking uncomfortable. I can't help it; a wave of happiness washes over me as I see him. When I left him at the airport I thought I may never see him again, and here he is, less than a week later, in my childhood home! It's surreal. I kiss him hello, and then quickly pull him out of the kitchen into the relative safety of my room.

"I can't believe you are here!"

"I can't believe you left me alone with your mother!" He looks shell-shocked, and I apologize profusely.

"I'm so sorry! I didn't expect you to be here so soon, and I panicked! How bad was it?"

"She ate me alive, spit me out, and then trampled on me for good measure." I stare at him wide-eyed, appalled, until I see his eyes crinkle in amusement.

"Just kidding."

I punch him on his arm playfully. "You got me! Sheesh, for a second I thought she killed you and I'm talking to your ghost. But seriously, what did she say?"

"Oh, what you would expect. That I should let you go if I care for you, because you have to find your own way in life. That this opportunity in Wales is great, and I shouldn't stand in your way. That sort of thing."

Hmm. Sounds like she went easy on him.

We talk for the rest of the day. *Really* talk. I know my side of the story, but not why he behaves the way he does. His viewpoint is surprisingly simple: there is not a single doubt in his mind about our relationship. We are *together*. Our fights and disagreements didn't shake him the way they shook me—"That's little stuff, compared to everything we have. It's the little hiccups you have to go through when you learn to live with another person." For him, we are in it for the long haul. Him and me, together forever.

He is hurt and feels betrayed by what he regards as my "abandonment."

At some point, he says, "If getting married is so important to you, then let's get married. I don't want to live without you!"

Well, when it comes to proposals, it may not rank high on the romance scale (like, at *all*). But hearing that makes my heart sing!

However, I gently point out that I am about to start a job in three weeks. I can't just bail on it, and I don't want to. If he really wants us to be together, he will have to wait.

"How long?"

"A year?"

That's been my vague plan, to give it a year while figuring out what to do with my life.

Richard looks crestfallen. I'm not thrilled about it either, so I make him a deal: I will work there for a minimum of six months. We will stay in touch, talk on the phone, and see if we have what it takes to make it long-term.

I don't mention marriage again, and neither does Richard.

We will have to take it one day at a time.

Chapter 22

WALES

On August 30th, I fly to London, take a train to Newport, and then a cab to the hotel.

The hotel looks amazing: it's a majestic building on top of a hillside, overlooking evergreen rolling hills and the town below. It's as imposing as a medieval castle, and when I stand in front of it, gazing up at the grandiose façade, I feel tiny and insignificant. I take a deep breath, and then step into the awe-inspiring lobby. My instructions are to go to the front desk, where I will be directed to my room.

A young desk clerk greets me with a smile. "Welcome to The Celtic Manor Resort! How may I help you?"

I explain that I'm a new employee, starting in two days, and that I'm looking for the staff accommodations.

"Name?"

I tell him, and after some rapid typing on his computer, his face brightens.

"Ah, there you are. You will be in the Manor House, lucky girl! Let me call you a porter, he will bring you there."

Two minutes later, a smartly dressed porter arrives and takes me to my new home: The Manor House.

It's the building where the hotel originated, which was first used as a maternity hospital before being turned into a hotel. It's stunning: dark wood, sweeping staircases, intricate wallpaper, expensive oriental rugs, and heavy draperies make it look like a castle fit for nobility. I have to remind myself that despite being treated like a guest right now, in two days I will be one of the servants, expected to treat the guests like nobility. I've never had to do this before, and I wonder how difficult it will be.

My room is small, but beautifully furnished. The window faces the low-pitched roof of the adjacent restaurant and the back road, with fields in the distance. It's a nice room, but it's still a hotel room, and once the porter has left (after an awkward moment of not knowing whether to tip him or not—I didn't, because wasn't he a colleague? But I still feel like a cheapskate), I don't know what to do with myself. It's the middle of the afternoon, and I have another 40 hours before the beginning of my first shift.

(Counting the hours will become an unfortunate habit of mine; almost like I'm a prisoner, I count the hours each day until the end of my shift, until the end of the day, until the end of the month.)

After I've unpacked, I decide to get to know the hotel better. My room is only a short walk away from the convention centre, my future place of work. At least I will have the shortest commute ever! I wander along a wide, carpeted corridor, past large picture windows, peeking into doors left ajar, trying to get a feel for the place. It's quiet, with no functions going on, and I try to see myself hurrying along these corridors in two days' time. It seems unreal.

Two days later, it becomes real. At five minutes to 7 a.m. I walk the short distance to the convention center in a knee-length black skirt and black, low-heeled shoes as instructed. The first thing I get is the rest of my uniform: a starched white shirt, golden vest with paisley print in the front, and a matching tie. I sheepishly admit that I don't know how to tie a tie, and one of my new co-workers makes a Windsor knot for me; I will keep that knot in my tie for the entirety of my stay.

What astonishes me the most during my first day is the stark difference between "the front of the house" and "the back of the house." The hallways behind the conference rooms are as far removed from the elegant guest areas as you can possibly imagine: the floors are concrete, and the walls are spattered with stains I can't place that first day; later I will learn that they are food stains, from when staff flings plates against the walls (which happens more frequently than you would expect). The same applies to staff: they are polite and courteous in the front, but as soon as they pass through the doors to the back, their vocabularies change drastically. The Welsh are fond of the word 'fuck,' and use it in almost every sentence when they are out of earshot of guests.

When they are happy to see you: "I haven't seen you in a while! How the fuck are you?"

When they are angry at someone: "That fucking wanker!"

When they want to emphasize a point: "You won't fucking believe what happened to me!"

As a compliment: "You are fucking gorgeous!"

As a verb in its original form: "I fucked her last night."

Fuck is used with much greater creativity in the UK than in Canada. I'm impressed.

Other words I'm soon learning are the aforementioned "wanker" (jerk), "mingen" (gross), "shite" (shit), "fanny" (lady parts), "tosser" (douchebag), and "shagging" (having sex).

Another phrase that's much more versatile than I ever knew is "piss off"; piss off means to get lost. If you're angry, you're "pissed off." But if you're "pissed," you're drunk. I have to restrain myself from taking notes, to not look like a complete tosser. It's a lot to take in!

I also learn that the Welsh have dinner at noon and tea at supper time. I find that one confusing, and try not to get them mixed up.

The day shift entails setting up tea- and coffee-stations for morning meetings, setting up buffets and food stations for lunches, and getting the dining rooms ready for sit-down dinners. Once the food service starts, we are serving, clearing away used dishes as quickly and unobtrusively as possible, and refilling food when necessary. During the evening shift, we fold hundreds of napkins into fancy shapes, polish glasses and silverware, and then serve during dinner and clean everything up afterwards.

We work ten-hour shifts, but the evening shifts are often longer, depending on the length of the function that is going on. The work is exhausting. The convention centre is huge, with only one kitchen, and we have to walk long distances every day. We are obsessed with how much we walk, and many of us tuck step counters inside our skirts to measure our steps. A normal day shift is usually between 10,000 and 20,000 steps, but during a busy evening shift, this number can easily double. Almost all the girls wear plain black flats, including me, but our supervisor bravely (or stubbornly? I can't decide) comes to work in three-inch heels every day.

While the work itself isn't that great, I'm endlessly fascinated by my co-workers. It's a mixed bunch: about half of the employees are from the

Czech Republic, Poland, France, Australia, or Canada. The rest are Welsh. I've only ever worked with Germans before, and I'm thrilled at this new experience. The English language is a great unifier!

Because many of us are here without our families, we're becoming a tight-knit group quickly. Not only do we spend most our waking hours together at work, we also go out afterwards often.

As I did in my high school-days, I'm once again hanging around the outskirts of several groups, instead of being a solid part of one. I don't do this on purpose; it's just what comes naturally to me.

There are the Canadians: most of them are from the same school I went to, but from the diploma-course instead of the certificate-course I took (which was even more expensive, and resulted in the same entry-level position I got. This is where everybody starts out, no matter if you spent thousands of dollars on a college education or not. I can't decide whether that's the way of a hospitality career—starting at the bottom and climbing the ladder—or if we were ripped off by the school).

The Canadians are sweet; I regularly meet two BFFs at the gym, where we usually sweat it out on the elliptical or the treadmill. (Well, *they* go on the treadmill. I despise it, and refuse to go on it unless all the elliptical *and* the rowing machine are taken. You know you have a problem with running when you prefer the rowing machine to the treadmill.)

I can't quite explain why I work out in addition to all the walking I'm doing, except for that I'm still screwed up about my weight, and since I'm sort of living the life of a single girl (without really being single), I feel it's part of what I should do.

Besides, have you ever lived and worked in a hotel before? If not, let me tell you: it gets old fast. TV sucks, there is no library close by, and this is still the age BE (before eReaders). I don't even have a computer! What else is there to do?

The Canadians all live a floor above me, and regularly hang out in each other's rooms. They repeatedly invite me to join them, but I rarely do, feeling like I might intrude.

Then there are the Polish girls. They are outrageous, outspoken, and very, very kind. Whenever we go out, I usually stick to them, because not only are they great fun, they are also tough and know how to take care of themselves.

Because if there is one thing I learn quickly, it's this: the Welsh are rough. They have hearts of gold, but during my first night at a club I witness two fights, hear about a stabbing in the men's room, and see two girls bitch-slap each other because the one girl made out with the other one's boyfriend.

I'm shocked, but our Welsh companions just laugh and assure us that it's all "in good fun."

"The lads are just blowing of steam. They'll be best mates again tomorrow, don't you worry!"

When they see my worried expression, they slap me on the back and tell me to "lighten up, love!"

The Polish girls don't live at the hotel, but share a flat in town. A few times I go to parties at their place, which involve copious amounts of vodka, dancing, and talking about "later." Few of us intend to stay here long-term; for many, it's a means to explore the UK, or to earn money to send back home. Despite being paid minimum wage, many of the Polish workers send money to their families. They do this by picking up extra shifts, working overtime whenever possible, and spending little money on themselves. I like and admire them a lot.

During one of those talks they ask me about my story: how did I get here? How long am I planning on staying? Do I have a boyfriend waiting for me somewhere?

I don't have an answer for these questions. Do I have a boyfriend?

Richard and I talk on the phone daily. We are telling each other about our days, talk about the kids, the farm, and mutual friends. In many ways, it's just as familiar as it's always been. We are still close. He's my person. I feel very much committed to him. He's still the first person I want to tell when something good or bad has happened.

Getting to my room after my shift to call him is the highlight of my day.

But we haven't really discussed what we are going to do. He tells me that he loves me. I know that I love him. Is that enough?

He is soon coming to Wales to see me.

And then we will decide what we are going to do.

When I pick him up at the airport a few weeks later, I'm startled at how much weight he has lost. We haven't seen each other for ten long weeks, and I have been so busy pretending how independent and strong I am, that I didn't realize how terribly I missed him until I'm embraced by his strong arms.

"Oh God, I missed you so much," he whispers, hugging me so tightly it almost hurts.

"Same here," I respond, kissing him at first gently, and then more passionately on the lips.

Someone whistles and calls, "Get a room!" but we don't care.

"No worries, we will!" I call back, and then laugh out loud. I'm so happy he's here!

I take him to my room at The Manor House, his home for the next week. I managed to get five precious days off, and I'm excited to show him around.

But that first evening is spent in bed. I smuggle in some food from the staff dining room, and we share a bottle of wine I bought just for this occasion.

And then, we talk.

He tells me how hard the last few months have been. Even without saying a word, I can tell; he is gaunt, with dark circles under his eyes, and he looks desperate.

"Miriam, it's been hell since you left. I can't live like this any longer. I will do anything if you just agree to come back. What do you want? What are we going to do?"

I lean in close, pull his face towards me, and murmur, "Just commit to me. And I'll be yours forever."

"I have always been committed to you," he says quietly.

He tells me how scared he is of getting married again.

How difficult it was to go through the divorce, knowing that he won't see his kids as much as before.

He tells me how heavily the financial burden weighs on him.

How painful it was to become alienated from friends because of the divorce.

I hold his hands and listen, not interrupting him. Richard doesn't talk about his feelings often; he needs to let it all out.

Then he says, "But you know what? Being separated from you is even worse. I hate it. This is the worst time of my life. Will you come back to me?"

I want nothing more. *Nothing.* It's so tempting to just say yes, fly back with him in a week, and "figure it out later." But we have been there before—which is what brought us to this point. I need to make sure that we will figure it out *now*, not at some unknown date in the distant future.

"Are you willing to marry me?"

Oh, the romance is off the charts! But I don't care. As the Brits would say: *Sod it.*

I'm sick of hoping for a romantic proposal that may never come; I need to know now.

"I'll do anything to have you back with me."

So, on a rainy Wednesday night in November, in a hotel room in Wales that's my current home, we decide to get married. We discuss the future, a wedding date, and a prenup; I insist on getting one, not only to put Richard's mind at ease, but also because I'm not in this relationship to get his money. I'm determined to become financially independent from him.

"Tomorrow, we will buy our wedding bands," Richard promises.

"I love you!" I say happily, hugging him exuberantly.

He kisses me tenderly and whispers, "I'll never let you go again."

The next day, we catch the bus into Newport to go ring shopping. We are headed to a small, elegant shop in the heart of Newport. I have looked at the display window many times, but I have never stepped a foot inside.

Today, I open the door confidently and lead Richard into the charming interior.

The bell tingles, and not even five seconds later a small, rotund man bustles through the curtain separating the front from the back, as if he was waiting for us.

"Good morning," he greets us effusively. "How can I help you?"

"We are looking for wedding bands," I tell him, unable to hide my excitement.

"Wonderful, just wonderful," he enthuses. "May I offer my sincerest congratulations?"

He extends his hand, and we both shake it, a bit taken aback. Neither of us expected that—but it's nice. More than nice; he's the first person to officially congratulate us! As soon as I realize that, I become choked up.

Tactfully, he seamlessly carries on. "What were you thinking of? Gold? Platinum? Silver?"

I look at Richard questioningly. We haven't discussed what we want, and I don't really care that much.

"Gold?" I ask him.

"Gold," he confirms with a smile.

"Excellent choice," he says approvingly, pulling out trays from the display case in front of him.

For such an important decision, we are done surprisingly fast. We try on maybe five different rings before settling on what we want: simple, heavy gold bands. The jeweller suggests engraving our names and wedding date in the rings, a suggestion we both like. Since we haven't set the date yet, we will come back later for that.

After the successful ring shopping expedition, we go to my favourite pub to celebrate. It's carpeted, has a huge fireplace, pictures of rolling country scenes on the dark-paneled walls, and not a single TV in sight. The atmosphere is homey, as if you are in someone's living room, and they have hearty, stick-to-your-ribs food that's to die for. As we're clinking glasses, I raise the question that's been on my mind since our engagement the night before. "When are we going to tell our parents?"

"I think we should do it as soon as possible. The sooner we get this show on the road, the sooner you can come home!" Richard is thoughtful for a moment, and then he brightens. "Hey, how about we fly to Germany and tell your parents in person?"

"What, *now*?" I ask doubtfully. I'm hesitant, suspecting that they will be anything but thrilled.

"You think that's really necessary?" My initial inclination is to tell them on the phone— or better yet, in a letter. I'm not big on confrontations, and I'd like to take the coward's way out.

Not on Richard's watch, though. "It's the right thing to do," he says firmly, and knowing that he's right, I reluctantly agree.

The following day, we fly to Germany. Once at the airport, we rent a car and then drive the three hours to my old hometown, where we check into a hotel. Our plan is to get a good night's sleep, and then surprise them the next day.

But first, there's a surprise waiting for me!

At breakfast, Richard takes my hands in his, and says gravely, "Before we see your parents today, we have to do something. Something very important."

"What?" I ask, having no idea what he's talking about.

"I have done this ass-backwards. The most essential piece is still missing."

"What?" I ask again, not getting it.

"We're engaged, right?" he says, looking at me expectantly.

I look back at him blankly.

He gives up. "I'm buying you an engagement ring today, silly girl!" Richard exclaims with mock exasperation. "Did you think I would introduce you as my fiancé without a proper ring?"

Who knew that this silver-bearded man of mine would be so romantic suddenly? I can't quite believe the transformation, but I won't look a gift fiancé in the mouth. I guess we're going ring shopping again! Twice in three days—it must be a record. Jewellery stores, here I come!

Three hours later

Okay, full disclosure: I don't think I'm a jewellery-person. I've been standing in front of one display case after the other like a fool, not knowing what I want.

"Which cut do you like?" the heavily made-up clerks ask me helpfully, and all I can to is shrug my shoulders helplessly. Cut?

They proceed to ask me about colour (aren't all diamonds white?), about clarity, about settings. I look at them dumbly, with no idea of what they are talking about. This is a foreign language to me, and I'm quite overwhelmed. Choosing wedding bands was so much easier!

To be honest, all the engagement rings look similar in my opinion. Sure, some have bigger diamonds and others have smaller ones, some have little diamonds clustered around them and others don't, but in the end? It's all sort of the same to me.

Plus, now that we're getting married, I keep a critical eye on the price tags, and I *know* that we can't afford to spend thousands of dollars on a ring. Besides, none of them 'speak' to me, or call out to me that they are *the one*.

Eventually, we've gone to every high-end, hoity toity jewellery store in the city. I've talked to all the over-powdered, over-perfumed sales ladies I can handle in a day (or a life time), and I'm ready to throw in the towel.

Since we are in town, I decide to show Richard our stall at the market place where we sell our produce twice a week. Who knows when we will be back next?

I take him there via small, lesser-known back alleys and side streets, because I want to get away from the crowds of people. One block away from the market place, I spot a tiny, funky-looking jewellery store that I have never seen before.

"Hey, look at that!" I call out, intrigued. Looking into the window, my flagging spirits rise again—these are some cool, unconventional pieces!

"Let's go inside, okay?" I say, not waiting for an answer, but opening the door.

As soon as I step into the store, I know that I'm in the right place. The girl sitting behind the counter is absorbed into crafting a piece of jewellery, just briefly looking up to say hello, and to instruct us to let her know if we need help before returning to her work. After all the over-solicitousness of the day, this is a refreshing change.

So is her look: she has short, spiky hair in a vivid shade of red; multiple piercings in her face and ears; a heavy smoky eye; and not a trace of powder *anywhere*.

I look at the many display cubes along the walls, and my heart lifts further—this jewellery is awesome!

And then I spot it. *My* ring. It's an open gold ring, with a small diamond on one side, curved on the other. It's simple, pretty, and totally *me*. I show it to Richard. "What do you think?"

"It's beautiful. Do you want to try it on?"

"Yes, please!" I beam. The girl must have overheard us, because she's already on her way.

I show her the ring I like, and she smiles widely. "I made that one. It's one of my favourites," she tells me. She carefully takes it out of the case, and hands it to me. Before I can slip it on, Richard takes it out of my hand. "Let me do the honours, will you?"

I look up at him, blushing as he carefully slides the ring onto the fourth finger of my left hand. It's an oddly intimate moment.

The ring fits perfectly.

"We'll take it!"

The only thing left to do is tell my parents. The last time we were all together, my mom told Richard in no uncertain terms that he should leave me alone. How will they react to us getting married? I haven't informed them of our visit, to use the element of surprise to our advantage.

As we approach our store, the butterflies in my stomach are dancing a wild tango. Ugh, I'm so nervous! At least I'm not alone this time, because I have Richard by my side. Together, we can do this.

Through the glass door I see that the store is empty, which means that they are in the back. I use my old trick of avoiding the bell by pushing the entry door open just wide enough to squeeze my fingers through to pull the exit door open. This way, we can sneak in unannounced. I put my finger to my lips, indicating to Richard to be quiet, and we both walk noiselessly to the back kitchen.

"Surprise!!" I yell, and jump into the room, Richard entering more dignified behind me.

Four heads swivel towards us, eyes wide, mouths open in an 'oh' of surprise: Mom, Dad, Oliver, and Emma. Looks like the gang's all here!

"Miriam!" Mom recovers first, and gets up to give me a hug. "What are you doing here? Is everything all right?" Her gaze travels from me to Richard, and I can see her initial confusion, before realization dawns on her face. She wasn't born yesterday; she knows what's going on. For a moment, a strong emotion crosses her features—anger? Disappointment? But it's gone in a flash before I can be sure what it was.

"Yes, everything is fine. Better than fine, we have news! I wanted to tell you in person, that's why we flew over last night." (No need to tell them that I didn't want to tell them in person at all.)

I look at Richard to gather extra strength, before blurting out, "We're getting married!"

Silence.

Then: "Are you sure?"

"Isn't this a bit sudden?"

"Have you thought it through?"

Aah, just the reaction you are hoping for when announcing your engagement.

We assure them that yes, we are sure; no, it's not that sudden, since we have been together for two years; and yes, we have thought it through.

The first one to congratulate us is, curiously, Oliver; he slaps Richard on the back and then turns to me, giving me a quick, stiff hug. The rest of my family seems to realize that the train has left the station, and belatedly follow suit. Emma wants to see my ring, Mom is talking about champagne and a special dinner tonight, and Dad is quiet.

It's awkward as hell, which is not surprising, considering I sprung this on them with no warning whatsoever. To give them some time to digest the news, I tell them that we have some things planned for the afternoon, and promise to be back tonight for dinner.

At dinner, my family uses a new strategy that pleases me enormously: grin and bear it. They seem to have decided that if they can't beat us, they may as well join us, and my parents offer to organize the wedding for us. Hurrah!

We discuss the size, location, and date of the wedding, and by the end of the night, it's decided: we will have a civil ceremony in my home town, with a small lunch followed by coffee and cake afterwards, with only family and four close friends in attendance.

Nothing about our wedding is special, but the date of it is. It will be on January 10th, exactly two years to the day when I first moved to Canada.

Is it strange that we sit around the dinner table, with my family barely knowing my fiancé, my parents disapproving of our relationship, my ex and my sister a married couple, all of us planning our wedding and pretending this is normal?

You bet it is. But nothing about the last five years has felt normal, and I'm beginning to think that this absurd, strange reality we're finding ourselves in, is *our* normal.

Maybe normal is overrated.

Or maybe, people everywhere are crazy, and are just pretending to be normal?

Chapter 23

UP TO MY OLD TRICKS

January comes, and with it our wedding day. I wish I could say that it was the best day of my life, but—well. You remember, don't you? The awkward pauses, too-short skirt, the thinly-disguised disapproval, the whole Monday-morning-ness of it all—it wasn't exactly a dream wedding.

But it's not the wedding that's important, it's the marriage, and I'm astounded by how great it feels to be married. Seemingly overnight, our relationship has gained more respectability. Is it my imagination, or are people taking us more seriously, now that we have tied the knot? It definitely feels that way. Being married also solves the problem of what to call Richard—introducing him as 'boyfriend' never felt right, and 'partner' makes me cringe. But 'husband'—now, that has a ring to it! I love it.

Three days after the wedding, I return to Wales to finish the last two months of my job. Richard flies back to Canada, impatiently awaiting my return. Before leaving Wales, my co-workers throw me an epic goodbye-party, and my boss writes me a wonderful recommendation. He also includes a personal note, which is heartwarming and humbling. While I can't wait to return to my husband, I'm grateful for my time in Wales. Not only did I learn a lot about a new culture, but I also learnt that I can make it on my own in a strange country. Before, I wasn't sure—after all, I have Richard's help in Canada. Knowing that I can stand on my own two feet boosts my confidence and makes me stand a bit taller.

Now I'm back, and it's wonderful. Almost losing the love of your life does wonders for a relationship. We treat each other with a newfound tenderness and affection, aware of how close we came to losing each other. We know that we won't let that happen again.

And there's more good news: I got my landed immigrant status!

Now that I have my paperwork in order, I can finally look for a job. There is only one problem: what do I want to do? The most obvious choice would be in the hospitality industry. After all, I spent $8,000 on a certificate and just returned from an overseas job at a hotel. It shouldn't be hard to find another hotel job. However, I'm reluctant to do so. Every time I picture myself in a serving job, my insides are screaming. I don't want to do it! Perusing the newspaper, I find myself drawn to an old faithful: retail. I apply for several retail jobs, and then I wait.

When the call comes, I'm in the middle of painting the kids' bedroom. Can I come in for an interview today? I assure them that I can, and then ask again for the name of the store, since I applied at several different stores.

"You're calling from…?"

"Parson's Farm Market."

Damn. It's them. I applied at the farm market on a whim, not seriously considering working there. I mean, I'm the one who swore to everyone who would listen that I would never take over the family business. I was the one who couldn't wait to get away from the farm market at home! And now I'm going to an interview at another farm market?

I don't have to take it, I tell myself. I can just go there, listen to what they have to offer, and then decline the job. Yes, that's what I'm going to do! It will be good interview-practice.

I show up there, resume and letters of recommendation clutched in my sweaty hand, inexplicably nervous. Why am I nervous if I don't even want the job? I can't help it—as soon as I'm in a performance-driven situation, I want to do well.

The manager leads me into an office that's so small, our knees would touch if I wouldn't consciously keep mine out of her way. She looks over my resume, seems pleased at my extensive previous experience at my parent's market, and then asks me some questions.

Reverting to my childhood need to please, I do my best to answer everything as perfectly as I can. I must have done well, because at the end of the interview, she offers me a job—as a veggie cleaner. Instead of politely declining like I'd planned, I hear myself saying, "Yes, I'll take it! Thank you so much!"

My new boss leads me to my future work area, a big sink in a window-less room with a garage door, which is open on this warm summer's day. My job will be to clean the veggies, stack them in the veggie display in the morning, keep the display replenished throughout the day, and mist them regularly every thirty minutes. At night, I will take it all off and put it in the cooler, followed by thoroughly cleaning the display case.

All that for $8.00/hr, which is the current minimum wage.

Instead of running away screaming, I nod along automatically, like my head is attached to invisible strings being pulled by someone else. Surely this is not what I want? Why am I saying yes to this job?

It's not until I'm back home half an hour later, having agreed to start in three days, that I ask myself, "Why the fuck did I do that?"

Is it nostalgia? Foolishness? The lure of the devil you know versus the one you don't? I have no explanation. Still stunned, I tell Richard that I got a job.

"You will never believe where," I tell him. Before he can make any guesses, I blurt out, "I took a job as a veggie cleaner!"

Seeing my desperate face, Richard laughs and opens his arms. "Come here. It's not that bad! I started out as a car washer, remember? It's your first job here. You work it until you've figured out what you want to do, and then you'll find something better. But you got one! It's better than nothing!"

Hearing him say that makes me feel better.

"You're right," I agree, nodding into his chest, this time completely voluntary—no invisible strings attached. "It's only temporary."

Famous last words?

When I show up at the job three days later, it's a boiling hot day. My effort of trying to wear something smart, but not too stuffy, fails spectac-ularly—the simple black top I chose is deemed too low-cut by my boss. My mortification is through the roof, but luckily, there is a solution: a work uniform. I'm being handed three t-shirts with the store logo, plus two sweatshirts to wear on colder days. I quickly slip one of the t-shirts on, and then we start.

Anna, the girl I'm replacing, shows me the ropes. She's twenty, and about to head to university, which is the reason for her leaving. I feel uncomfortably old and inferior in comparison. Am I moving backwards? This job is for high school or college students, not twenty-five-year-olds who have their shit together. But that's just the problem: I don't have it together. It's my first job in this country, and in many ways, I feel as unprepared and intimidated by the real world as a sixteen-year old starting her very first job. I tell myself to stop comparing my situation to other people's, and to make the best of it.

After being a veggie washer for several weeks, one of the cashiers quits, and I'm being promoted to cashier. With the promotion comes a raise; I'm getting one dollar more per hour. Yay! Being in the front raises my status, and the other girls start talking to me more. It's not like they were unfriendly before, but I wasn't "one of them." Now, I am. We joke and laugh together, and occasionally, they go out for drinks or dinner. The first time I'm invited along feels like a huge victory. I belong somewhere! While most of them are in their late teens or early twenties, the supervisor isn't. She is in her thirties, and when we start getting to know each other, we find out that we have something in common: we are both stepmothers.

She is the first person I meet who is in a similar situation to mine! It feels incredible. With this shared commonality, we bond quickly. We start hanging out regularly after work, and when the husbands meet and like each other, I feel like I won the lottery.

A year goes by. I'm now twenty-six years old, and I'm still working the job that was supposed to be only temporary. During the winter, when I have to return to washing veggies because they are short, I almost quit, because I can't handle having my hands in the cold water all day. They hurt like crazy and I'm freezing all the time, and one day, I have a meltdown at work and tell my boss that I can't do it anymore. She is sympathetic and understanding, and we have a long, honest talk about my prospects at the store. I tell her that I'm not sure what I want to do, but that I didn't plan on staying at the store long-term. But I like it there, because it's safe. Comfortable. In my more insecure moments, I ask myself if maybe this is all I'm good at? If maybe it's in my blood, and I'm kidding myself if I think I should do something better?

After our talk, my boss surprises me further: she offers me a position they created just for me, as assistant manager. Not only am I touched by the kind gesture, I also wonder if it's a sign. Am I meant to stay there?

The job duties are a bit murky, since they never had an assistant manager before. There's the manager, and my friend who is the supervisor, and now there's me. Over the following weeks, it becomes clear that there are too many cooks in the kitchen. A tension that never existed before develops between me and my friend, compounded by the fact that I know, deep down, that I don't want to spend the rest of my life there.

My next step is clear: I have to figure out what I want to do.

This is easier said than done. I suck at knowing what I want! However, by now I've had to face the sad reality that there is no magic fairy waving her wand and giving me my dream life—I'll have to figure it out by myself, like everyone else. After much thought, I come up with a plan. What I need is a deadline, a list, and much more information than I currently have. It's the middle of the summer, and I give myself until the beginning of the new school year to come up with a career plan. It's a tight schedule, but I know that, like most people, I only get stuff done under a certain amount of pressure. The next step is the most important one: a list of everything that's important to me about a job. I have never sat down and written out my requirements and preferences, and once I get started, it becomes clear why I have been so unsuccessful in finding a satisfying career thus far. I've stumbled around blindly, hoping to accidentally come across my dream job. I'm not good at math, but even I realize that this approach has a laughably poor chance of yielding the desired result.

Well, it may be late, but it's never too late!

My list includes everything from the hours I want to work, to the job security, to the level of responsibility, to income, to how much I'm willing to work with other people. Taking these requirements into account, plus everything I've learnt from my previous jobs, I come up with this list:

- Work to live, not live to work (my parents serve as cautionary tale for that one)

- Work inside (Forestry taught me that in a hurry)

- Have a job that includes both sitting and walking (sitting on a desk all day makes me sleepy)

- Make enough money to not have to worry about it, but not so much that it becomes stressful

- Be part of a team, but also work alone on occasion

- High job security

- A job that leaves plenty of free time

- An education that doesn't take forever. I'm approaching 27, I don't want to go to school for an eternity

Once I have finished my list, I talk to everyone I know about what they do for a living. Some of our friends are retired, and I have never asked them what their jobs were.

One of our close friends used to work in Medical Radiography, a term that means nothing to me.

When I research it online, I learn that this job—x-raying people— ticks all the boxes on my list. Huh, working in a hospital; the thought never crossed my mind.

Could I do that?

While I'm still mulling the idea over, two things happen that help me make the decision. The first one is Richard. He has been a champ throughout it all, being as supportive as can be. The only thing he won't do is my repeated request to "just tell me what to do!"

"Oh no, I won't fall into that trap," he tells me firmly. "I don't want to be held responsible when it doesn't work out. Besides, I don't know what you would enjoy. You'll have to figure that one out by yourself, babe."

However, a few weeks after that conversation he does give me a helpful hint, if inadvertently. He has an appointment for a chest x-ray, and upon returning, he mentions in passing, "That would be a good job for you."

Shortly after that, our friend Owen visits us. As luck would have it, he also had an x-ray recently, and without prompting, he tells us how he talked to the technologist about her job, her income, and how she likes it.

"Miriam, that girl was raving about her job. They make great money! Aren't you looking for a career change? Have you considered that?"

Is it a coincidence? Or do you believe in signs?

I don't know if I see signs because I keep looking for them, or if they really happen to help me along. It doesn't matter. I take these two unrelated, eerily timely occurrences as hints that I'm on the right track.

Calling or not, I make my decision: I will become an x-ray technologist.

Chapter 24

BACK TO SCHOOL AGAIN

Leaving the agony of indecision behind feels amazing. I'm so excited! However, I come crashing down from my high when I find out what the requirements for attending school are: at least 75% in Biology, English, Math, and Physics. If you think that doesn't sound that hard, you are a better student than I was. Because I have none of that. And I suck at Math and Physics! Another hurdle is the fact that approximately 600 students apply for the program every year, and only 80 are being accepted. These are *not* great statistics. And I'm pretty sure that most students' first language is English, giving them yet another advantage I don't have. My spirits sink even lower. Am I being realistic here? Maybe I should just give up and work as an assistant manager for the rest of my life?

But somewhere deep inside me, a steely determination that's usually nowhere to be found wakes up.

It's the same determination that made me face my parents and tell them that I'd drop out of college to move to Canada.

The determination that made me move to Wales when I thought I had no future in Canada.

That determination gives me a stern talking-to. "You'll never find out when you don't try it," it tells me. "What can you lose? If you fail, you can continue to work in your current job if you want to. You won't have lost anything. But what if you don't fail? What if all that stands between you and a great job is only your fear and insecurity? Are you willing to risk that?

Don't be defeated before you have even tried."

Richard is either a mind reader or in cahoots with my inner voice, because he gives me a pep talk that's uncannily like my determined inner voice.

"You are one of the smartest people I know," he begins. He's my husband, so he has to say that, but it still does its job: it makes me feel better.

"Look how quickly you learnt English!"

Not that quickly, I'm thinking, but I'm not pointing it out. He's on a roll; no need to make him stop.

"You have an inner fire and determination that will make you achieve anything you set your mind to. If you want it, you can do this!"

Gosh, he's good at this encouragement stuff. Not only am I feeling great by this point, but I'm starting to believe him—he's *that* convincing. Not for the first time, I reflect how awesome marriage is. It has your personal cheerleader built in!

The next year passes in a flurry of activity: I sign up for all the required courses at a secondary school while still working full-time. There are many days where we barely see each other, because we're both working so much.

But it's worth it: I get into college on the first try!

Three weeks after my twenty-eighth birthday, I start my third college career. Will the third time be my charm?

At first, it doesn't look like it. I quickly realize that this college is not at all like the quaint Tourism college. While I was the star student there, here I'm struggling. I have difficulty getting used to the exams, overthinking the multiple-choice answers, and getting them wrong frequently because I suspect they are trick questions. The first mark I get is only 65%, while everybody around me seems to have aced their exam. I promptly burst into tears, which is mortifying enough in front of people, but when the teacher notices and asks me to come into her office after class, I feel like I'm going to die from embarrassment.

She tries to be helpful. But when she hints that my mark might be due to a language barrier, I feel even worse. Not having adequate language skills is my biggest fear. Am I doomed? I've been speaking English for five years, and I don't feel like I'm missing any context or meaning when I read, write, and speak it. But maybe I do? Maybe I only *think* I understand it, all the while missing important subtleties?

Am I not cut out for 'real' college? Am I kidding myself? This possibility is too awful to contemplate. I extricate myself from the office as quickly as possible and flee, to get away from the teacher and this terrifying thought.

Luckily, I'm not alone. I've bonded with two other students, Magda and Ben, and the three of us do everything together: going to lectures, doing group projects, having lunch. Magda is Ukrainian, and smart as a whip; she's a straight A student, and she takes it upon herself to get my grades up. Ben is the total opposite, seemingly unconcerned with grades and school work, just doing the bare minimum to scrape by. His nonchalance (and poorer grades than mine) make me feel better, and with Magda's help, Ben and I slowly get the hang of it.

Apart from Magda and Ben, I don't socialize much with the other students. I feel awkward being back in the student environment at almost thirty, and to be quite honest, I find most of my fellow students weird, which doesn't bode well for the future—after all, these are my future co-workers.

At the end of the first semester, I have my first clinical rotation—which is awful. The technologists at the hospital either ignore me and the other student, or are condescending. We both find those five weeks difficult, and by the end, I'm seriously worried that I made the wrong choice once again.

I wonder if this is how people get stuck in lives they don't like: have they taken one wrong turn too many? Do you give up at some point? Is there even such a thing as a dream job, or is that a myth?

Despite my misgivings, I'm determined to see this through. I'm not sure if it's stubbornness or pride, but I need to finish something. I can't be that girl who has a new job every few years, always blaming others when it doesn't work out.

Also, this career checked all the items on my list, and I have to trust *the list*. If *the list* is wrong, then everything I believe to be true about myself must be wrong, too—and if that's so, what the hell am I supposed to do?

So, I stick with it. Fortunately, it gets easier. I become friendly with a few more students. The subject material starts making more sense. And the best part is, when I have my second clinical rotation six months later, I really like it. Finally! I'm so relieved, I want to cry. Maybe I didn't choose wrong after all?!

There are three major differences to the first site that make my second clinical so enjoyable: it's a small site, in a small town, and all my co-workers are at least twenty years older than me. They are nurturing and supportive, and only too happy to share their accumulated wisdom. I learn a lot, and become much more confident than I was before. Halfway through, one of the technologists tells me that I'm doing a great job, and that comment makes me float through the rest of my practicum. Kindness to others goes a long way! You never know how much someone else might need it. That's one of the many lessons I'm learning during this practicum—probably the most important one.

When the staff give me flowers and a card on my last day, expressing their hopes that I will come back one day, I have to fight back tears. In that moment, I know that I'm on the right path, and these wonderful people gave me that gift.

I will never forget it.

The last year of my education arrives, the majority of which will be spent working in two hospitals. The first hospital is great: the staff is kind and supportive, and they make us students feel welcome and included.

The second one is a different story. On my first day, the person who was supposed to show me around isn't there, and nobody seems to be willing to step in and take over. I stand around awkwardly for a while, until one of the elderly employees takes pity on me and gives me a short tour. It's over before I know it, and then I'm left alone.

I quickly find out that there is a clique at work that includes about half of the girls working there. They stand around in little groups, whispering to each other, and stop whenever someone outside the clique approaches. Me being a student, there is no chance that I could ever become a part of them, and it often happens that I walk into a room and find two or three other technologists there, talking urgently to each other, looking annoyed at my interruption. I take the hint and leave, feeling like a bad smell comes off me. It's an awful feeling, and doesn't make for a pleasant work environment.

Once again, I don't fit in. I'm not part of the group.

I shouldn't care about this stuff. After all, I have the best husband! And great step kids! And we have our circle of friends, who, miraculously, have now accepted me. Even Richard's best friend, who retreated for a few years, has returned to us. First the marriage, and then my career choice in health care, must have convinced him and his wife that not only are we the real deal, but I also don't seem to be a gold-digger. Ha! The unspoken gold-digger accusation always makes me laugh. If they would know how much a divorce costs, they would never make such a silly claim. The only way to get money out of married guys is to keep them married!

Divorces are expensive. Why? *Because they are worth it.*

But that's beside the point. I want to have a happy career, and these bitches might very well be my future co-workers. Why don't they like me?

My only consolation is that the other students don't fare any better. We meet regularly for drinks, to decompress and complain about the hardship that is being a student in a working environment. You have to work harder than anybody else, and are being judged harsher than anybody else. It's not fair! But, as my mom is fond of pointing out, life isn't fair. Hence the drinks- and bitch-sessions.

However, time, the great healer of most problems, also works in my favour. The closer we get to our finishing line, the friendlier the formerly bitchy girls get. One of them confides in me about a fight she had with her boyfriend over the weekend.

Another one complains about her boring family dinner, and how she'd rather have watched *Survivor* instead of enduring her family. I can sympathize with that wholeheartedly.

So much, in fact, that I can *almost* forgive her for completely ignoring me the week before, when she was talking to some girls from the clique, and I made the mistake of trying to join into the conversation. All of them completely ignored me, which is an unpleasant experience when you're standing right next to them, less than three feet away. Upon realizing that everybody did their best to ignore me, I awkwardly stopped speaking mid-sentence. It was horrifying.

But all is forgiven when something incredible happens: I'm invited to one of their infamous girls' nights I have heard about, but was never a part of.

It's just a few weeks before graduation. I have worked alongside them for six months, becoming increasingly more independent and confident in my abilities. On a Wednesday at shift change, the girl I secretly call 'queen bee' approaches me.

"A few of us are going out for drinks this Friday to Cactus Club. You should join us!"

I almost fall over with incredulity. Inadvertently, I look over my shoulder, just to make sure that nobody stands behind me. Is she really talking to *me*?

Yes, it appears that way. She looks straight at me, and as if reading my thoughts, confirms, "Miriam, are you interested? We would love to see you!"

"Yes, I'd love to! Of course, I'll be there!" I babble, my words tripping over each other in my effort to convey my acceptance of this spectacular invitation. Omg, how did this happen?

It doesn't matter. Don't look a gift horse in the mouth! All I know is this: I will hang out with *the girls* this Friday.

A lot of effort goes in my outfit-selection for this momentous occasion. In fact, an emergency trip to the mall is in order to find something suitably fashionable and trendy. I buy an off-the-shoulder shirt, something I've never worn before, but I feel I have to give it my all. This is an audition: an audition for acceptance into the girl group. I may be a bit different, but I'm no fool. They know that the boss is going to hire me as soon as I'm graduated (he's mentioned it several times in front of everyone), and they're testing me to see if I'm worthy to be recruited into their hallowed ranks.

I go all out. Not only am I wearing my sexy off-the-shoulder shirt, I also put on my tightest pair of jeans, highest pair of heels, and make-up (minimal for others, major for me: mascara, eye shadow, lip gloss *and* blush). I also do something different with my hair; I usually wear my pixie parted at the side and down, but tonight, in a reckless moment of thinking "all or nothing!", I spike my hair up in a daring imitation of Halle Berry's best short-hair-moments. It feels radically different—appropriate for the occasion. Will tonight change my social standing forever?

My heart is pounding when I leave the house. This seems *very* important. There have been many momentous occasions throughout the last ten years.

Meeting Richard. Deciding that we want to live together.

Telling my parents. Meeting his kids. Meeting his friends. Leaving Richard (one of the hardest things I have ever done). Moving to Wales. Getting married. Becoming a Canadian resident.

Here is another one. They never get easier, do they? This one seems just as important as all the ones before. *I want this.* I want to be accepted by my peers. I don't want to be the odd girl out forever. Can I be one of the girls? I don't want to be special any more. All I want is to be *normal*. To be accepted. To be one of them.

This is my chance.

Will I make it?

Chapter 25
TO BREED OR NOT TO BREED? THAT`S THE QUESTION

Oh My God. I did it! I'm *in*! For the first time since my middle school days, I'm part of a girl group again. We greet each other effusively every time we meet, with hugs and high-pitched exclamations about how amazing we look.

"You look fantastic!"

"Your dress is so cute!"

"Your outfit is to die for, you have *the best* style!"

"Your make-up is flawless, you're the queen!"

"Omg, did you lose weight? You look so skinny!"

I feel out of my element, not used to overly gushy behaviour, but I adapt quickly. I'm dying to fit in, and maybe that's how all girl groups behave? How would I know? I haven't been part of a girl posse in fifteen years, I'm hardly an expert.

Not only do we work together, but we also text after work daily. A few of the girls are obsessed with the show *Jersey Shore* and live-text when watching it, and in the name of fitting in I give it a try, but I can't bring myself to watch these idiots. Apparently, even a desperate people-pleaser like me has her limits.

But for everything else, I'm game! We get pedicures done regularly, a new experience for me, but one I love. We also go for coffee, work out together, and a few times we organize girls' nights. Real girls' nights out, with getting all dolled up, having cocktails before, and behaving in a raucous and ridiculous manner. I'm on a high. The feeling of being just like everybody else is exhilarating. The best part? They're all active on social media. Not only do we have a great time while we are out, but there are photos to prove it.

One of my friends is a talented photographer, and she often brings her camera along for photos of us. While I find posing for them stressful (because I can't pose for the life of me, and feel like a big, clumsy ogre in comparison to them), I can't wait to find myself online. After a night out, I check my phone manically every five minutes, impatiently waiting for her to post the photos on Facebook and Instagram. She is a kind person who only posts flattering pics, and once they're up, I'm in heaven.

Look at me, world! Here I am, part of a girl squad, just like the rest of the cool people!

For a while, everything is going well. We're having fun! One of my biggest concerns since I was a child was not having friends, and I feel like I can confidently cross this item off my life's to-do list. Just look at my Facebook profile! I'm young, I'm part of a girl posse, and thanks to filters (Filters! What a genius invention!), I look pretty. Do I still feel like the odd-one-out? Yes, frequently. While the other girls wear Ray-Bans, Lulu-lemon, and Michael Kors accessories, I buy my clothes from Old Navy and have never spent more than $20 on sunglasses. While they all have long, flowing hair, love their make-up, and are no strangers to fake eyelashes and hair extensions, I have ultra-short hair and feel fancy when I put on a touch of mascara and a wee bit of eyeshadow. But I'm part of the gang. I am. Right? *Right??*

Richard and I have couple friends, but do they count when they're never displayed on social media? Looking at me online, you would think I'm friendless. Most of our "adult" friends don't even have a Facebook account!

When the first friend becomes engaged and starts talking about bridesmaids, I become obsessed with the idea of it. I'm already married and shouldn't worry about it, but seeing how other weddings ('real' weddings in my mind) are planned, I feel more inadequate than ever. Not only was my own wedding about as far removed from a white-gowned, bridesmaid- and groomsmen-filled big affair as it could get, I also can't stop thinking about the question of bridesmaids. If I would have had a *normal* wedding, whom would I have asked to be my bridesmaids? At the time of my wedding, I didn't have any best girlfriends.

One of my friends makes a snide remark about a girl who asked two of her co-workers to be her bridesmaids, commenting that "she doesn't have any real friends." The unkindness of that statement shocks me, because I feel that, until recently, I was in the same boat.

This isn't the only crack that's starting to show. Increasingly, I feel uncomfortable around them. For a long time, I can't put my finger on the problem; all I know is that I don't feel like myself around the girls. But, desperate to fit in and to be *normal*, I try to ignore my feelings and pretend that everything is fine. Fake it till you make it, right?

That is, until I'm confronted with a topic every single woman will have to deal with in her life: the baby question.

All my friends know that they want kids. I'm not sure whatsoever.

In contrast to them, I have been a part-time stepmother for most of my twenties.

While they have been living carefree lives that allowed them to focus just on them and their boyfriends, I've cooked a Thanksgiving dinner for eight when I was only twenty-three and barely knew how to cook.

I hosted an Easter celebration for thirty people the following year, making bunny-shaped goodie bags for ten kids and preparing food and drinks for thirty.

I hid from the disapproving glares of the mothers when picking up my young stepdaughters from school three times a week.

I watched cartoons with the kids at 7 on Saturday mornings, while my friends probably got home only hours before and would be in bed till noon.

I baked cookies, and made lunches, and taught them how to knit, subsequently spending many evenings in front of the TV, all of us happily knitting away on our scarves and potholders.

I know the powerful relief you feel when, after a week of having them every day during summer break, their mother pulls up in her silver Toyota Corolla like a knight riding in on his white horse, and picking the kids up for *four whole days*. Oh, the sweet freedom! Having time to yourself! Not having to answer a million questions, or making the millionth meal, or coming up with activities for them to do!

Obviously, I feel enormously guilty about having these thoughts. I may 'only' be a stepmother and not a 'real' mother, but I have the mother-guilt *down*. A+ in the guilt department!

My point is: I've been doing the kid-thing for ten years. Only part-time, and they are not my flesh and blood, but they feel like my kids. And the nagging, unwelcome thought niggles away in the deepest, darkest recesses of my brain: I don't think I want to do it again.

But what does that make me? What kind of horrible woman doesn't want children? Particularly since I already have stepchildren, and don't I see how rewarding that is? If I don't, then something must be wrong with me.

And there it is again, my ever-present fear: I'm afraid I'm not normal.

I love the kids. And I wouldn't trade the time we've spent together for *anything*. Children are fun and rewarding, and having these girls in my life has made it so much richer.

But kids are also exhausting. They are always *there*. If I'd have my own, it wouldn't be a part-time gig, with another woman doing the mother-load of the mothering; it would be all me, baby. And I don't know if I want that.

But, once again, I'm the odd one out. Everyone I know seems to want babies. And as if that's not bad enough, I seem to give off a powerful signal to the world that screams: ask me about my baby-plans! Suddenly, barely a day goes by where someone doesn't ask me when we'll have a baby.

"When are you and Richard having kids? Don't wait too long, seeing how old he is."

"How old are you now? Thirty-two? It's time to get started soon, isn't it? You don't want to be too old!"

Oh yes, our ages are brought up frequently.

When I voice my doubts that I'm not sure if I want to have kids, the parent brigade is quick to point out that I'm wrong.

"If you don't do it, you'll regret it later!"

"Having children is the most rewarding experience in the world."

"Who will look after you when you're old?"

"Men come and go. Our children stay with us forever!"

"You looked after Richard's kids, you deserve to have your own."

"You would be such a great mom!"

"You haven't experienced true love until you have your own baby."

When I look doubtful, they seem to adjust their opinion of me. I can almost see how I'm losing several notches on the approval scale, because a woman who doesn't want to do what she was born to do is not to be trusted. After all, isn't bearing children our duty as women? Aren't all females born with the desire to procreate? A woman who doesn't have that desire is faulty. Something about her is broken.

And what about all the women who desperately want children and can't have them? They would kill for having my healthy uterus! (Assuming mine *is* healthy. I haven't put her to the test.)

While I have managed to mostly avoid pregnant women in my life thus far, suddenly that's not possible any more. My co-workers start breeding, and it seems to be catching; more and more fall pregnant. Is there something in the water? Every single pregnant lady is being celebrated like she is the first expecting mother in the history of the world. Everybody is so excited! People hug them and jump up and down with glee, even the ones that couldn't stand each other BP (before pregnancy). That's all changed now—pregnancy unites them. It's like joining a club, and as soon as the sperm burrows into the egg, you are a member. No men or unfertilized eggs allowed!

Whenever someone at work gets pregnant, the news is being told and re-told for weeks, and when I can't muster the required enthusiasm, people look at me strangely. Am I gaining a reputation as the weird girl who hates children?

The thing is, I *don't* hate children. Most of them I like quite a bit, and some I even love! Like my stepdaughters and nieces. I also understand completely why people want kids. Creating a new human with your own body is freaking *awesome*. There's also the whole science-experiment vibe attached to is, of wanting to find out what happens when you mix one person with another. And kids can be fantastic! Unless they are assholes. Don't pretend you don't know what I'm talking about; asshole kids exist.

So, I get society's obsessions with children. What I want is a *break* from the kid-question. Just leave me alone for a while! But nobody is giving me a break. Every magazine I open features another celebrity holding her little bundle of joy in her arms, saying things like, "I thought my career was important, but this is the most important job in the world for me now!" or, "Being a mother is the role of a lifetime!" Ugh.

Every pregnant woman in my vicinity sparks the same question: when will I be next? And if not, why not?

It seems that a woman's womb is not her private business, but public property. Every person seems to be entitled to an opinion about what she should do with it. You're fairly safe when you're in your twenties, with the public opinion having come around to the thinking that there is 'still plenty of time.' But once you've hit the big three-oh, the fun is over. It's time to grow up and start breeding!

My friends are completely on board with it. They start talking more and more about *when* to start their families instead of *if*, and with them I can't just walk away—I have to be supportive.

But I feel lonely in my uncertainty, and I wonder: would it really be so bad to have a baby? A baby with Richard's blue eyes and my freckles, and little companions right from birth in the form of my friends' kids? Swimming against the stream is so exhausting, why do I keep doing it?

Maybe all the other people are right, and I'm wrong. Why not give up and give in?

Would that really be so bad?

But I'm not the only one to make this decision. My husband is the other affected party, and he is approaching sixty rapidly. From the beginning, we agreed that if I really wanted a baby, he would give me a baby. "I want you to have everything you want," he promised me. "I have kids, I would never want you to miss out on the experience if you want it."

We have been together for ten years, and we never seriously considered adding our own to the mix. Now his children are almost grown up. We are both looking forward to the time when we're having more time for each other. My friends are in their thirties, with another forty or so years together—but we don't have that luxury. If we are lucky, we have twenty good years together. And if we have a baby, it will never be just the two of us again.

However, this is all noise. Good points, yes, but they are skirting around the essential question: do I want to become a mother?

The uncomfortable truth is: no. I have no desire. I could talk myself into it, or do it to make other people happy, or even do it to fit in and appear normal, which is a *terrible* reason.

But the fact remains: I have no desire to have children of my own. And I'm all alone with this decision.

Then the first one of the girl gang becomes pregnant. It's Alex, the resident photographer and party girl, and part of the inner circle. Our group started out with Regina, me, and Alex, and the rest was added on later, as what I secretly consider the outer circle. Regina, Alex, and I frequently do stuff without the others, like going for walks, working out, or having lunches and dinners together. I'm so grateful for our friendship that I included a photo of the three of us in a collage of family, friends, and pets, and put it up on our living room wall.

Now Alex is preggers, and Regina is beside herself with excitement. All she wants to talk about is Alex's pregnancy. She buys Alex a gift the first time we see her after the announcement, and since I show up empty-handed, she offers to say that it's from both of us. Instead of feeling grateful, I feel terrible. Did I break one of the many unspoken rules I don't know about? Was I supposed to buy an announcement-gift? When did life become so complicated? And why do I feel so strange inside? Not jealous, but lonely. Despite trying so hard, it seems like I will never fit in.

When they put their heads together and talk excessively about pregnancies and babies, I have nothing to contribute. I feel completely left out, and, even worse, like a selfish, terrible friend. Why can't I be happy for Alex? It's not like I want a baby myself.

It takes me a long time to realize, but what I'm grieving for is the short time I had where I felt like I belonged. Now, with my friends making the shift from being carefree women to becoming mothers, everything will be different. They will become members of the mom-club.

And I won't.

Chapter 26

BLOGGING IT OUT

For a while, I keep pretending. I listen patiently to endless talk about the many side effects of pregnancy. I listen to the members of the mom club gush about what it's like to be a mother. I go to baby showers, trying not to show my dislike of the games played there. I keep having to answer (or deflect, depending how strong I am that day) questions about my own baby plans. I smile through the loneliness.

What I can't figure out is *why* I feel so lonely. I'm happily married, I have a good relationship with my step kids, I like my job, and I have friends. Where does the dissatisfaction come from? Why do I feel, deep down, as if I'm disconnected from the world?

As always when I'm unhappy, I retreat into the world of books. Reading has been my most faithful friend and saviour since the age of six, when I learnt how to read. Ever since that time, absorbing myself into someone else's story has given me a reprieve from my problems when I need to escape reality for a while.

In addition to books, I discover something else: blogs. It's the year 2013, and blogs have been around for a while, but as usual, I'm late to the party. Reading people's thoughts and following along on their life journey is fascinating! I feel like I have discovered a new world, one in which people are open and honest, and write about stuff I would never dare talk openly about. Or would I?

Without thinking it through, I decide on a whim to start my own blog. An irresistible force is drawing me towards this intriguing concept: to write about one's life. Normally, I don't jump into something head first; I think it through, rethink it, and then think some more. I'm a true overthinker, which often results in me *not* going for it. If you think long enough about something, you can always find reasons why it's safer not to try it. It's too scary, you might fail, it's a lot of work, it has the potential to be embarrassing…the list of reasons goes on and on. But this is different. I'm powerfully drawn to this concept of 'blogging' and decide to just go for it. I google "how to start a blog," get a Blogger domain—and then I start. Saying that I have no idea what I'm doing is an understatement. I know so little about this new world, it's laughable, and I also don't know anyone personally who blogs. But something about it just feels right. Writing about what's going on in my head is therapeutic, and to my surprise I realize that writing down my confusing thoughts helps me to make sense of them.

I'm hooked. In the mornings, I jump out of bed instead of my usual hit-snooze-twice routine, brimming with energy and fresh ideas for the blog. It's not only that I'm addicted to writing; it's also that after a while, I'm starting to find women like me, women who have made unusual choices, women who decide to stay 'childfree' (a term I have never heard before), and women who are not afraid to dream big. I'm not alone! It's a revelation.

For all my life, I've looked only at my immediate surroundings for inspiration and guidance. It just so happened that the people who live and work with me were different from me—not lacking or wrong, just different. But having nobody around to share my specific experiences and troubles with made me think I was wrong. Was I broken for lacking the instinct of wanting to have children? Was it weird that I craved so much alone-time? Did other people think that our marriage was strange—and even if they did, why did I care? Why didn't I have a BFF like other girls? Why was I so angry sometimes? And sad or confused at other times? I didn't have a reason. Surely, one needs a reason to feel such strong negative emotions.

For the first two years of my blog's existence, I write a lot. Writing helps me to unlock my soul, and slowly, gently, I unearth stuff I was afraid of facing for the first time in my life. I'm motivated by other people sharing difficult truths, especially when they say afterwards how liberating it feels. Admiring their courage, I wonder if I could be like them: afraid, but doing it despite the fear. Can I be brave?

I try it out by writing about something that I have always felt deeply ashamed of: my struggle with depression. About six months before starting my blog, I have begun to take antidepressants, which help me tremendously. But like many people with depression, I don't talk openly about it. Richard knows, of course, but barely anybody else does.

One morning I wake up, feeling daring and a bit reckless. I make myself a cup of coffee, and then sit down with my laptop and start typing. The words flow easily, as if they have been waiting to finally come out.

"I have been thinking about writing about this issue for a long time. Since last October in fact. Since I didn't have a blog then I wanted to open up about it on Facebook, but didn't have the guts. It is very personal, and it is easy to come up with a ton of reasons not to do it: "it's private," "nobody is interested," "I don't want people looking at me differently."

The reason I decided to do it anyway is that I got help last October and it changed my life completely.

I hope that this will help some of you to summon up the courage to do the same—it is SO worth it!

I suffer from depression.

Thinking back, I would say it started right around the onset of puberty when I was 14. But the most memorable and horrible time when I first realized something was wrong was when I was 18. On the outside, everything was fine: I had a boyfriend I adored, fun friends to hang out with and party, was liked by my teachers in school, earned my own money to be able to buy the things teenagers like (mainly clothes—for me it was always about clothes).

It was the time where you have to figure out what to do with the rest of your life, and I didn't have a clue, but neither did my friends, so I wasn't too stressed out about it.

But what I remember vividly was that all the things I liked to do—reading, partying, meeting my friends, rollerblading—suddenly lost their appeal to me. I didn't enjoy anything anymore. A deep hopelessness settled over me. I had this strong feeling that everything in life is pointless. The world is a horrible place. Planning for the future? What for?

I felt so alone. Was searching for a reason why I felt so sad and hopeless, was hoping something horrible would happen in my life so there would be a reason for this awful feeling.

Depression didn't occur to me. I had no Internet back then to google my symptoms (which is what I would do now), couldn't talk to my parents since they didn't understand, didn't even think about going to my doctor (what would I tell him?), didn't know where to turn.

So, I suffered. That bout of depression lasted a long time, a few weeks, but eventually faded with the approaching summer and I started to feel better again.

Fast forward a few years: now I'm in Canada, living with the love of my life. Things are good.

On the outside, I look like a happy, bubbly person. I am a happy, bubbly person.

My outlook on life is very positive—I always expect good things to happen, strongly believe that if you want something, visualize it, work towards it, then it will happen.

But still...

This feeling of sadness wouldn't leave me alone. I might be totally fine for weeks, and then suddenly I'm overwhelmed with sadness. Would start fights with my poor husband.

One example: I had a good day at work, everything was fine. I get home. There are a few dirty dishes on the counter. And from deep inside me I get this overpowering anger, taking over my whole body, turning me into this mad, screaming, stomping mess.

Richard knew all along, he has experience with depression in his family. He urged me for years to seek help, but I thought I can control it by doing yoga, reading self-help books, positive affirmations. Mind over matter.

It doesn't work that way.

Finally, last year, after a vacation where I cried every day and was deeply unhappy, he sat me down and told me that our marriage was in danger if we didn't seek professional help.

Together we went to my doctor and I told him all about it. The mood swings, sudden bursts of anger, the sadness. He was amazing! Listened, and understood. Told me how common it is (a third of his patients have depression!). Oh, the sweet relief!

He explained to me that the most likely cause of my depression is a chemical imbalance in my brain: a shortage of serotonin, a neurotransmitter. No level of positive pep talk can boost serotonin levels. It's a chemical imbalance that can be solved with a drug that boosts serotonin levels. He prescribed me an anti-depressant: Citalopram, also known as Celexa.

The effect of this drug has been life-changing. And I don't use this term lightly.

The internal turmoil is gone! What before felt like a stormy sea where I was helplessly thrown up and down, is now calm. Peace. Harmony. It's incredible!

When I talked to my doctor, I said, "But I function, I have never missed work or stayed in bed all day."

And he responded, "I believe you. But life doesn't have to be so hard."

And that's exactly it.

Depression is still hard to admit to. It seems like a weakness, or a "luxury condition" of people who don't have real problems.

But it is a real illness. Thankfully, it can be treated with medication, therapy, or a combination of the two.

The reason for this post is that I hope and wish that someone will read this who feels the same way I used to feel; know that there is help and you can feel a million times better! Don't wait almost 20 years like I did before getting help.

Life is too short."

When I'm finished, I show it to Richard and ask him if I should really publish it.

He reads quietly, and when he is finished, he nods approvingly and says, "I think it will help other people if you do."

"They feel alone, too," it slowly dawns on me. "If we all hide our truths, people everywhere will feel the way I have for most of my life—alone, like freaks, like something is wrong with them." I take a deep breath, and then, my heart pounding wildly, I hit "publish." I can't quite believe that I have put on the Internet that I have depression, and that I'm taking antidepressants! Am I insane?

But then I get the responses. And they are heart-warming, honest, and wonderful. Many people from work read my blog, and they come up to me, telling me how relieved they are that they are not the only ones.

One co-worker gives me a hug, and says, "I never thought you would have, you know," she hesitates.

"...Depression?" I smile, finishing the sentence for her.

"Yes, exactly!" she says relieved. "You seem so happy and full of life all the time!"

"So do you," I counter. "That's just it, isn't it? If we don't start talking about it openly, it will never lose its stigma. I am happy a lot of the time, but not always. And when I'm not, I think I have to hide it, because it's a flaw that nobody should see. We have to stop doing that! We should treat mental illness like, let's say, the flu. Nobody is ashamed to say they have the flu, right? Well, sometimes we get a bout of depression, and feel emotional, or sad, or raw, or dead inside. It sucks, but that's the card we have been dealt. Not our choice and not our fault. And nothing to be ashamed of."

The more I blog, the more I get to know myself. It's shocking how little self-awareness I've had for most of my life! I'm thirty-four before I realize that I'm an introvert. Having grown up with highly private parents, I wanted nothing more than to be an outgoing, fun-loving girl. I was desperate to be the life of the party, everybody's best friend, the one everybody likes.

My personal history has shown me again and again that I'm not like that. But I wanted it so much. I fought so hard to be that girl, and was disappointed every time I 'failed.'

Now, I'm finally starting to accept who I am: a flawed woman who is scared a lot, brave sometimes, full of love and life, but also filled with insecurities, weaknesses, and a surprising tendency to swear when you least expect it. Can I learn to like her? Will I ever *love* her?

With the budding self-awareness comes the recognition that I don't want to be friends with one of the girls anymore. The friendship has become hard, and complicated, and full of potential traps I unintentionally fall into all the time, which makes me always worry that I may say or do something wrong. After hanging out with her, I often feel worse than I did before, and surely that's not the purpose of a friendship? No Instagram photo is worth that sacrifice.

Besides, I don't want to pretend any more. I want to be true to the person I am, and show the world exactly who that person is. No masks and lying necessary.

The 'break-up' isn't easy. I hate confrontations, because it plays on my biggest fear: that the other person will throw into my face everything I'm afraid of hearing, which is that I'm a horrible person and that nobody likes me. I remind myself that I'm stronger than this, that it doesn't matter what other people think, that I have to be okay with the person I am and nobody else.

We have a brief, unpleasant text-exchange—and then it's over. I'm so relieved, I could cry! Instead, I laugh and hug Richard fiercely, who is behind me all the way. Who has been behind me from the day I met him. I look at his face, a face I know as well as my own, and I'm struck with the realization that as long as I have him, I have everything I need. He is my best friend, and he accepts and understands me like no other person ever has before.

I don't need the validation of other people. I have my man who loves me, and I'm beginning to be okay with the person I am.

I feel like I'm waking up from a long dream. It's a dream that was pleasant at times, but that turned into a bit of a nightmare towards the end. It was distracting, had the potential to be destructive (I dodged that bullet, phew!), and it didn't bring me one step closer towards living my best life. But I have learnt many lessons, and I'm grateful for everything that happened.

Some friendships are meant to last a lifetime; this one wasn't.

Now that this chapter is over, I can focus on the one question that has occupied me all my life: what exactly do I want to do with the rest of my life?

Chapter 27
CHASING THE DREAM

"If you would win a million dollars in the lottery, what would you do?"

"A million isn't much. Once we've paid off the mortgage and all our debt, we would only have a few hundred thousand left."

"Okay, ten million then. Or a hundred! Just play the game, will you? I want to know what you would do if you'd have all the money in the world. "

Richard looks up thoughtfully into the canopy of the willow tree, taking a sip of his drink. It is summer, and we sit in our favourite spot, playing our favourite game: what we would do if we had no money worries.

"Well, I would probably buy more land," he begins. "And then get some cows to put on the land. Go on a few vacations a year? Well, not more than two, I like being at home."

"What else?" I ask him, idly stroking Snowflake, one of our dogs. It's so comfy in my hammock, and I have my eyes half-closed, listening to Richard's soothing voice.

"Hmm, I don't know. Not much else, really; I'm happy the way we live. Aren't you?"

"Oh, I am!" I assure him. "I love it here! I don't think I ever want to leave this place."

I open my eyes and look around at our little paradise: the swans gliding gracefully over the pond; a gaggle of geese resting by our feet, unperturbed by the sleeping dogs next to them; the horses grazing in the field to our right.

"Well. Until the rain starts," I amend, and Richard nods. We live on the west coast of British Columbia, also known as the 'wet' coast, and our winters are mild, grey, and very, *very* wet. Once the rainy season starts, we are trudging through mud for about seven months, getting soaked to the skin every other day. The summers are spectacular, but the winters? They are wearing on us.

"Okay, my turn," I say eagerly.

"If I would win the lottery, I would want us to move to the wilderness. Not totally cut off from civilization, just a few minutes away from it. No immediate neighbours. We would live in a little log cabin with a wrap-around porch, where the dogs can hang out. I would have my morning coffee on that porch every day, and the air would smell of pine trees."

I'm warming up to the subject, picturing it vividly in my mind.

"In front of the porch is the horse pasture. Our house is on top of a hill, so we have a nice view, and sometimes, in the early mornings, we can see deer grazing."

"No more wet winters!" Richard chimes in. "We will live in dry desert air, with cold, dry, and sunny winters."

"Snow on Christmas!" I add happily. "And sun every day!"

"I want to be able to ride off from our property, no horse trailer needed."

"And I can have the dogs off leash, without anyone complaining."

"No traffic noise."

"No traffic, period."

"I can sleep in every day!"

"I can write every day!"

We look at each other.

"Do you think it's ever going to happen?" I ask him.

"Who knows?" Richard says. "Crazier things have happened."

Considering that neither of us plays the lottery, our chances of fulfilling our dreams that way are zero. But for a strange reason, I'm not worried. I'm convinced that what's supposed to happen *will* happen, and all I have to do is relax, not stress, and keep my eyes and my mind open for any opportunities that may arise.

We like where we live now, and if we are meant to stay here, then it will be for the best.

However, I think about our dream place often, visualizing it as clearly as I can. I also write it down, including pictures of what I want the place to look like, to make it seem more real.

Whenever I picture ourselves in our wilderness paradise, I get excited. I'm careful to think in certainties instead of possibilities: we *will* move, instead of we *might* move.

I put it out there into the universe, and once I have, we lean back and enjoy our present life.

This includes visiting our friend Patrick. He and Richard used to work together, until Patrick moved to a small island and retired. We have never been there, which is why we are now making the trip.

The island is known for its green eco-vibe, organic farm markets, tiny house-culture, and sustainable living. It's a magnet for hippies, free spirits, people dropping out of the rat race, and anyone who is looking for a slower, more spiritual life.

Once we have caught up on each other's lives, Patrick asks us if we have ever been to a dance temple. Dance *what*? Apparently, it's a weekly event where people meet up to dance their hearts out. It's sort of like a disco, but less Flashdance and more Woodstock. It sounds fascinating.

"Would you like to go?" Hells yes!

Thus begins a night I will never forget.

We arrive at a modest wood building in the middle of nowhere, nestled into a forest with a small meadow in front of it where kids are running around like little wood fairies. They are barefoot, with long braided hair, wearing bell-bottoms and pretty, flowy tops. We pass a couple of outhouses (there are no other washrooms) before we step inside.

We are greeted by a sea of shoes on the floor, and Patrick indicates for us to take ours off as well—the dancing is to be done barefoot. We stand in front of a table that has a basket overflowing with 10- and 20-dollar bills sitting on top of it, and we pay our entry fee of $10.

The friendly girl who is collecting the money—she introduces herself as Naomi—has a banner of Tibetan prayer flags draped around her shoulders, and motions to the woman in front of me to step forward.

Naomi holds a bowl with incense in one hand, lights it and starts to wave the smoke all over the woman with an eagle feather.

I must look bewildered, because Patrick leans in and whispers in my ear, "She is being smudged. Have you ever been smudged before?"

"Can't say that I have," I whisper back. "What is it?"

Before he can respond, it's my turn. I hesitantly take my place in front of the smiling Naomi.

"Welcome," she says in a musical voice, "is this your first time?"

I nod.

"I will purify you," she explains, waving the smoke in my direction.

"Now is a good time to think of all the things you want to let go of. Stress, unpleasantness, anything that happened today that you didn't like—let it all go. Turn around."

She proceeds to tap me lightly with the feather on the head, moving down my body.

"You are done. Enjoy!"

Smelling thoroughly of incense now, I move into the dance room. And stop and stare.

There are about 60 people there, and they were *writhing*. There is no other word for it. One girl is lying on the floor, short dress hiked up above her panties, waving her arms in the air and moving her body rhythmically back and forth. Other girls are stomping their feet wildly, arms up in the air, hair flying. Several of the guys have their shirts off, sweat glistening on their muscular backs. The music is surprisingly modern, an electronic pop-mix that is fast-paced and quite catchy. I stand with my back towards the wall, taking it all in, waiting for Richard and Patrick to join me.

"What do you think?" he asks gleefully. Without waiting for an answer, he takes me by the arm and pulls me farther in. "Now, we dance!" he announces, and starts to boogie.

Richard and I exchange a look. A half-naked bearded man with long hair, several pouches slung around his neck and baggy jeans hiked halfway up his impressively large stomach, notices our hesitation and approaches us, burning stick in hand. He starts to wave the stick in front of us, smiling manically and blowing the smoke in our faces. Another smudging? I feel purified enough, so I slowly back away.

And then I start to dance.

The atmosphere is infectious: people lost in the music, eyes closed, whirling around the room without any inhibitions. There is a small stage at one end, which seems to be a make-shift yoga space. One girl is practicing handstand, another is stretching on the wall; a guy tries out some breakdance moves. There are also several little kids there, running around between the dancers and on the yoga stage.

In another corner is a small table piled with Tarot cards, crystals, incense, some books, and candles. And above it all, the music keeps on playing, and people keep on dancing, faster and faster. By now there are about 80 of us in there, and the room is packed. The smell becomes decidedly earthy; more clothes are shed.

What the...? I don't trust my eyes for a moment—are those bare breasts bouncing along in sync with the music? Sure enough, the first woman has lost her top and jumps happily around like a little elf, short hair sticking up, breasts freed from their usual confinement, wild and free. Before long, another one joins her, and then another. Soon there are five or six women dancing topless, completely unselfconscious. They are in the company of most of the men being shirtless, just wearing lose-fitting pants or shorts.

The light is dim, the air is hot and ripe, the whole tableau in front of me utterly mesmerizing and bizarre.

Suddenly, as if in response to an unheard signal, the dancers start to make a sound: unintelligible, swelling in volume, getting louder and louder. Starting out as a clashing mishmash of chaotic noise, their voices unite to turn into a harmonious melody of surprising clarity and beauty.

It is utterly mesmerizing. I have never witnessed anything like it, and despite feeling out of place, I can't help but also feel enveloped by a unifying love.

Oh God, I'm starting to think like them, I realize, and laugh out loud.

"What is it?" Richard asks me, and I tell him.

"Life is fucking beautiful, isn't it," I finish, and he nods. There is so much to see, do, learn, and discover, if we just keep our minds and hearts open to the world and all its wonders. I promise myself to be more receptive to new experiences. However, minutes later, I draw the line at where my receptiveness ends: at a sweaty, smelly, breast-squishing group hug in which our fellow dancers engage. Richard and I hastily retreat, opting out of that experience.

Our weekend on the island stays with me. There is a freedom and sense of peace to Patrick's life that I'm missing in our daily life. Both Richard and I crave more nature, less people, the goal that initially drew us to Canada. I'm even more watchful for any opportunities that might crop up, quietly signing up to a job alert system that will email me if there are any jobs available in the areas we have started to consider as new possible homes. We keep assuring each other that, "We are just looking. If it doesn't work out, we are happy where we are." But the seed is planted. I keep going back to the piece I wrote about what our dream place looks like, and I'm yearning for it. I want it. And there is something else. In the back of my mind, my story scratches on my insides—this story—reminding me that it wants to come out. It's been there for several years, and I have tried to ignore it, to reason it away. I told it to leave me alone and to go to someone with more talent and more experience.

And yet.

In unguarded moments when I'm feeling really good and confident, I see myself sitting by a window in front of my computer, typing away. This image is so vivid, I can feel it. Feel the keys under my fingertips, the sun on my face, my dog by my feet; hear the rustling of the wind through the open window. I can see the words forming in my mind's eye, and then transferring them from the confines of my mind to the page.

And my soul is telling me: do it. You know you want to. *Just go for it.*

The next year, the real estate market explodes. It's been steadily going up for some time, but until now, we never paid close attention to it. As long as the kids were still in school we never considered moving away, and besides, what about our jobs?

But the kids are all grown up and working, and now we are paying attention to the market.

'For Sale' signs pop up all everywhere, and when a neighbour puts his property up for sale, we ask him how much he wants for it.

"1.6 million," he says casually, and I almost choke on the apple I'm eating.

"Say again?" I ask, aghast. "I thought you just said 1.6 million."

"I did," he laughs. "I know it's crazy, right? I paid less than $300,000 for it, but that was thirty years ago. Times have changed!"

I'll say.

His property is the same size as ours, with an older house and similar outbuildings on it like we have.

"Should we find out how much our place is worth?" I ask Richard when we are alone.

"You read my mind, babe," he replies, and gets on the phone to find a real estate agent.

Two days later she comes, looks at everything, and then names a price. We can't believe it, and tell her that we have to think about it before we make a decision.

Over the next few days, we discuss at length if we could imagine selling our place. Sure, we have talked about it for years, but talking about it in an abstract way and doing it are two very different things. Do we really want to start over somewhere new? Leave the kids, our friends, my secure job behind? What about money? Are we ready?

"Do you think this is one of those chances we will regret not taking?" I wonder aloud.

"I think so," he answers. "Look at it this way: what's the worst that could happen?"

"We hate the new place. I don't find a job. Or I do find a job, and hate the people. We don't find new friends. We are lonely. We won't be able to move back, and we will be miserable." I rattle off without having to think about it. I'm an expert at imaging the worst.

"Or," Richard counters, "we end up loving the new place, you find a job you like even more than the one you have now, we find new friends on top of our old ones, whom we're not losing, since we aren't moving that far away. What if it's better than what we have now?"

"I guess that's a possibility," I admit.

I'm trying to get my positive attitude back, but fear is paralyzing me. Suddenly, all I can think about are all the things that could go wrong. Am I crazy for even considering giving up my job? What about retirement? What about Richard's business? What about our beautiful spot under the willow tree?

I'm freaking out. I need to change the tape in my head, and get away from that negative mindset.

Richard sees my stressed-out face, and gets us each a large glass of wine. When he's back, he sits down close to me, takes my hand into his, and looks me into the eyes.

"Miriam, I know you're worried. But remember what you and I have done together! Compared to what we've been through, this is nothing. We are in it together, and I'm not in the least worried. Just because we're putting our house up for sale doesn't mean that we have to sell. If we don't find a place we both love, we stay here. Nothing lost! I was just as worried as you are now when I sold my first house. But let me tell you: as soon as I was at my new place, I was fine. It will be the same this time. Trust me, okay?"

I do. I know that with Richard by my side, I can do and handle anything. This will be an adventure!

I remind myself of what I know to be true: we only regret the chances we didn't take.

God, photos are liars. Euphoria replaced my initial panic, but has since been replaced by a deep-seated mistrust for real estate photography. Those guys are wizards with a camera.

Judging from the photos, the first place we look at has huge potential: ten acres, a log home, and a large pond right by the house. I picture myself sitting on the covered deck with Richard in the evenings, sipping wine, watching the swans and ducks glide gracefully over the water, the dogs playing and the owls hooting...

"You can't keep any bird alive here," Richard states matter-of-factly, shattering this fantasy at once. "See the steep hill right behind the house? There is wildlife coming down from there in masses. They will kill everything."

Oh. So much for that.

Still, there can be a solution for that, right? Better fencing, covered enclosures, something...Optimistically, I head around the house. There is a small building behind it, a shed of sorts. Peering through the windows, I see what looks like living quarters: a two-burner hot plate, some clothes strewn about, boots on the floor, books on the walls. Upon a closer look, I realize that the shed is built onto a camper. Confused, I step back and look around. Is that a—*bath tub* over there? Sure enough, there is a bath tub in the grass a few feet away from the camper. A few two-by-fours have been nailed together as a make-shift privacy fence, shielding the tub from two sides.

Rich starts to laugh. "Somebody lives here, and we are standing in his bathroom!"

I wonder if he comes with the house?

Finally, we go inside. The first room we step into looks great: an open living/dining room with lots of windows, letting sun and light in. It has high, vaulted ceilings, and the walls, flooring, furniture, and stairs are all wood. It looks cozy and inviting. The kitchen is attached to the living area, and while small, it has windows all along the work area. I like being able to look out the window when I'm cooking, so I'm willing to overlook the size.

"Where are the bedrooms?" our real estate agent wonders aloud. There seem to be none around.

We start searching, and discover a covered hallway of sorts. It looks like a connecting walkway between buildings, the ones you see between hospital wings sometimes.

The thing is: this house isn't one building. It's two small houses with steep pitched roofs, on stilts, connected by the walkway-structure.

We enter the second house, and step into one big room. The room contains everything: a queen-sized bed in one corner, which is the first "bedroom"; a desk, couch, and coffee table in the centre of the room functioning as the office/living room; and a kitchen on the other side, with a tiny breakfast nook squeezed into the corner.

Our agent checks the listing, where it clearly states that the house has three bedrooms. Where are they? As we gaze around, Rich notices a ladder attached to the ceiling. It has a pulley on the side, and upon pulling it, the ladder descends slowly from the ceiling. We look at each other, bemused, and I climb up to discover a small loft that's completely bare. The owners installed a headboard on the side closest to the stairs, and I realize that when putting a mattress on the floor, it would look like a bed. Sort of.

The third bedroom is in the basement, and it's the only real bedroom of the house. It actually has a door you can close! There's also a shower around the corner, but that's it. Just a nook for a shower. No door, no sink, no space even to hang a towel. It's as if there was a recess in the wall, one you could use for shelving, or maybe a closet, and they decided to install a shower instead.

The entire house is a curious mishmash of beautiful details put in odd locations. Like the fact that there is a pretty claw-foot bathtub—in a tiny, window-less room that makes me feel claustrophobic. Nothing is straight, everything looks DIY, done by a creative genius with little patience for a measuring tape.

Thanks, but no thanks.

Just down the road is the second house. We know little about this place, aside from it being ten acres, because there was only one single photo. As soon as we lay eyes on the house, it becomes apparent why: the house is a tear-down. It's a wood shack, described as "partially remodeled and ready to be finished to your own taste." That's a wild exaggeration if I ever heard one. We almost don't even want to step inside, but figure we have come this far, we may as well take a look.

To reach the front door, you need to get over a ditch. How? By precariously balancing on a few planks nailed together, which creak ominously upon stepping on them. I feel a hard hat and steel toed boots would be a more appropriate attire than my sandals and long skirt. This looks like a construction site!

The agent knocks on the door, and we hear a voice from inside inviting us to come in.

We open the door.

The inside is dark. All the windows are covered with either cardboard or blankets, presumably to keep the house cool. As my eyes adjust to the gloom, I notice boxes upon boxes everywhere. There is no furniture in this room, just boxes and junk. A tiny woman of indeterminable age bustles in, greeting us. I can't help but think of the witch from Hansel and Gretel. She gives me the creeps.

Apparently, she was packing—I think?—because the second room also contains numerous boxes. We quickly pass through, into a dark kitchen. I barely look around, eager to get this tour over with. I do notice that this seems to be the room that's used the most, because it looks tidier than what we have seen so far. We poke our head into a sad little bedroom with peeling wall paint, and open the back door to stick our heads out. A tiny kitten darts away, and I feel bad for her for having to live here.

We say goodbye, and beat a hasty retreat.

"I wouldn't stay here if they'd pay me," Richard states, and I whole-heartedly agree. This place is horrible.

And so it continues.

I secretly hoped that we would find a place and just *know*. Fall in love head over heels, with no doubts, and live happily ever after.

But, it appears that life doesn't work that way. The 'perfect' place doesn't exist. I'm on an emotional roller coaster that alternates between hope and defeat, and it's exhausting.

When we get an offer on our place, we are thrilled—closely followed by panic. We still haven't found a new place. What if we never find one?

Chapter 28

LIVING THE DREAM

It's early. I quietly get out of bed, pull on my jeans and a sweater, and head outside to let my dog Lily out of the truck. We stayed the night at our friends' house, and later we will look at more properties.

Lily greets me exuberantly, as she always does, and we start walking. It's one of those magical early autumn mornings, where fog hangs in the air, slowly drifting about, the sun is starting to break through, and the sky above is a clear, luminous blue. I take in a deep breath and smile to myself. The smell is indescribably lovely. It smells of earth that has soaked up many months of hot summer sun, of leaves getting ready to change into their brilliant autumn colours, of fragrant pines, and a hint of cool, delicious mountain air that promises the impending bounty of the harvest season. It's my favourite scent in the world, and I inhale it deeply. As we are heading up the mountain, I gaze at the picturesque valley to my left. Soon, a house comes into view—one we have looked at a couple of weeks before, and haven't been able to stop thinking about since. It has many of the features we want: vaulted ceilings, plenty of large windows letting lots of light in, and a view that's to die for. But it also has neighbours on each side that are too close for our liking, and we have been holding out in case we find something better. But seeing the house now, sitting peacefully in the glow of the golden sunlight and shrouded in morning mist, a deep sense of belonging envelopes me. I can't explain it, but it feels right.

It feels like home.

Two weeks later, we buy it, and two months after that, the move begins. With the amount of animals we have, it's like a revival of Noah's ark, but with way more than just two animals of every species. We have to transport several dozen rabbit cages with about two hundred rabbits, hundreds of birds, and a wide variety of other animals: sheep, horses, llamas, guinea pigs, and dogs. The good news is that our new home is only a three-hour drive away; the bad news is that the road between the two is the notorious Coquihalla Highway, which has been dubbed as 'one of the worst roads in all of North America' in the winter. It's an extremely steep mountain road, and the mountain pass on the top gets very icy and snowy, which makes the road highly dangerous. And when are we moving? In the winter, of course. Having decided to forgo a moving company and do it ourselves with the help of our horse trailer and generous friends, we each drive the treacherous highway close to twenty times, lugging all our worldly belongings up and down the mountain. Separately, we each get stuck in a snow storm on one of those drives, with the visibility so poor that the world beyond the headlights is impenetrable blackness, and all we can see in the headlights is a crazy whirl of white snowflakes, menacingly hurling towards us and making us dizzy.

To make matters worse, I get food poisoning from dodgy Chinese food on one of my drives, with the stomach pain and snow competing to see which one can make my life more miserable.

To distract myself from the pain and panic, I start to sing Christmas songs at one point, only interrupting myself to throw up halfway through.

But we make it. On our first morning at the new place, we see a deer walking peacefully across our yard, in clear view of our living room windows. Windows that, come to think of it, overlook the horse pasture and the hastily erected sheep pen and the duck and goose run …

"Rich!" I exclaim in astonishment. "We have a house that overlooks our animals, just like we wanted!"

"You are noticing that just *now*?" he asks me incredulously.

Well—yes. Once we signed the sales agreement, time sped up, and I haven't had time to stop and reflect because everything happened so quickly. This clear winter morning is the first time in over two months that I'm taking a moment to really look around me, and I'm overcome with a deep feeling of gratitude.

Our new home is flooded with light. That's the first thing people notice when they step in our house. Its entire east side is made of windows, with a large deck attached to it, and we have beautifully sunny mornings almost every day of the year. Because that's the other amazing new reality of our life: we live in the semi-desert now. After a lifetime of wet and rainy weather, we finally live in a climate that is dry and hot in the summer, and dry and cold in the winter.

When the first snow falls ten days after we move in, we can't get over the transformation. It's the definition of a winter wonderland! With the ever-present sun and blue sky, the white landscape glitters as if a million diamonds are scattered all over it. It's breathtakingly beautiful.

Our friends Will and Kathy live close by, and when Kathy invites me to go cross-country skiing with her, I excitedly accept.

I'm instantly hooked. Gliding soundlessly over sparkling powder snow amidst majestic, white-capped trees is heaven. The first couple of times everything goes smoothly, and I smugly tell myself that I'm a natural at this sport. Sadly, our next outing ruins this illusion.

It's a grey and overcast day. Kathy and I are the only ones out on the trail, with one notable exception: there are paw prints on the track. They are from a cat, either a bobcat or a lynx. These beautiful creatures are not usually dangerous to us, because they will avoid humans if the can. But if they feel threatened, they can attack. I have huge respect (you could also call it fear) for all animals when I'm out in the woods, and it feels special—and quite unsettling—to ski along where a big cat has walked not long before us.

The snow is crusty that day. It has melted and frozen, and under a thin layer of fresh snow it's icy. Ice is nobody's friend, is it? Unless it's cooling my drink, I have no use for it. It's dangerous to walk on, drive on, and ski on. Nope, I'm not a fan.

What I don't know yet is that ice can also pack a mean punch. But I'm about to find out.

When you're new at cross-country skiing, going downhill is your nemesis. It's tricky to keep your balance, and more than once I have fallen over when going down a hill.

We are skiing down a particularly steep slope, and as I'm picking up speed, I start to panic. When I see a bend coming up, I have to make a split-second decision: should I try to make the turn, or give up and simply go straight into the deep snow?

I decide to go straight.

It's the wrong choice.

As I plow into the deep snow at high speed, something stops my skis abruptly, causing me to dive headfirst into the snow. It hits me like a brick.

The layer of ice under the seemingly fluffy white stuff punches me in the face with a force that is as unexpected as it is painful.

I lie there for a minute, stunned. Then I try to slowly make my way out of the deep snow, which is no small feat with long, cumbersome skis still attached to your feet and blood dripping everywhere.

Kathy comes skiing along, yelling and laughing. "That was a spectacular nose dive!" She abruptly stops laughing when she sees my face. "Oh my god, are you okay?" she asks me worriedly.

"It hurts like a motherfucker," I say, and she looks slightly shocked—I usually don't use that kind of language in front of her. It does hurt a lot, though. I've never been punched in the face before, and I can't say that I'm keen on ever repeating the experience again.

Kathy has a first-aid kit with her, and we slap a huge band-aid across my nose, where the bleeding is the worst. On shaky legs, I get up and gingerly test my limbs. Apart from my face, everything else is fine, and we start to head back.

I'm a little bit ahead, gliding carefully towards the parking lot, when it happens. Looking up from the trail to see where the car is, I spot the owner of the paw prints. A lynx walks soundlessly across the road, distinctive with his brown-grey coat, black ear tufts, and a short, stubby tail. He's gone in seconds, like a ghost, and for a moment I'm unsure if I saw him or imagined him. The encounter has left me breathless and enchanted. Good thing, too, because the shot of euphoria helps me cope with a sight that's a lot less thrilling: my face. Upon flipping down the visor and opening the little mirror, I get a shock: I have deep scratches across my nose, on my chin, and around my left eye. The eye is already beginning to swell up, and will bloom into an impressive black eye. I look like I was in a bar fight, and lost.

Richard gets a kick out of it, and laughs at me for a week.

Thankfully, the eye heals up nicely in time for my first day at my new job. I'm starting as an x-ray technologist at the local hospital. It's been five weeks since I worked my last shift at my former job, and I'm overjoyed that I found a new job so quickly. Upon announcing to my old co-workers that I was quitting my job without having a new one lined up, they swiftly proceeded to make worried faces at me, asking me repeatedly, "Are you sure you're doing the right thing? What if you don't find work? Have you thought this through?"

If you're a worrier by nature, this sort of talk does *not* help. But all the worrying was unnecessary, because here I am, working again!

I quickly fall in love with my new job. We live in a small town, where everybody knows everybody, and I stick out like a sore thumb (in a good way). Staff and patients alike are curious about me, and when they hear that we moved to town for good, they warmly welcome me. People are so friendly, I'm quite taken aback. Within days, everybody seems to know my name, and I try my hardest to repay the favour.

Then there are the patients. The first time someone tells me they 'got a horn to their knee' I'm mystified. Huh? When he elaborates and tells me it's from a bull, "because I'm a bull rider," I'm thrilled. All my childhood fantasies are coming true! This is a real cowboy town, and I'm quickly getting used to regularly seeing cowboy boots, enormous belt buckles, and cowboy hats. Soon, I don't bat an eye when an off-duty doctor walks in with his spurs on, clanging down the hallway to visit his patients before going on a ride with his horse.

In the spring, we hire a group of guys to help us build all the barns and chicken coops we need. They work hard, but they also like to have a good time. We get into the habit of sharing a beer after they are done for the day, listening to music and telling jokes. They are great guys, always in a good mood and upbeat.

When we ask them a few weeks later to help us get 700 bales of hay, they don't hesitate. We spend two hot and sweaty days picking up hay bales from the field, driving load after load back home, to stack them in the brand-new barn. When we are finished, we have a party in the barn, eating pizza, drinking beer, and singing along to the guitar one of the guys brought along.

The next morning, Richard and I are outside, feeding the animals. Our dogs follow us, playing and snuggling up close, putting their heads right into our hands, wanting to be petted. It's the height of summer, and the air is already warm; later, we will meet some of our new friends and float down the river on tubes.

As always, I pause under the cluster of pine trees for a moment, leaning against the fence and gazing over the valley. A few hundred yards away I can see two deer grazing peacefully. I breathe in the air I love so much: that delicious smell of warm earth, spicy pine, fresh hay, and a whiff of clear mountain air. I will never get tired of that smell; it's the scent of freedom and happiness for me.

Our next-door neighbours are in their yard, waving at us and confirming that we are coming over for dinner later. We have become good friends, an irony that's not lost on me, considering we thought we wanted to live far away from people.

Richard comes up from behind and puts his arms around me. I lean back into him, sighing happily.

"We are so lucky, aren't we," I say to him, something one of us says to the other almost daily.

"Yes, we are," he confirms.

Life is good.

EPILOGUE

Richard and I have been together for fifteen years. We have long ago silenced all the doubters, because being in a relationship that long can only mean two things: either we are *really* committed to proving everybody wrong, or it's true love.

The great thing is I don't care anymore what other people think of us. Richard taught me a long time ago that we have no control over other people's opinions; the only thing we can control is how we react.

He's not a teacher at all, this man of mine, but I always wanted to learn to see life the way he does.

It's just that he loves life so *damn* much. He is a master in making the best of what he has. He doesn't wait for his life to begin on that mythical day in the future when all his dreams come true—he's having a great time today, *right now*.

I wanted—no, *needed*—to know how he does it.

When Richard and I knew each other for just a few weeks, we were on one of our daily phone calls when he told me something that amazed me so much, I never forgot it.

"If I were to die tomorrow, I could honestly say that I've had a great life." I almost dropped the phone when I heard him say that. What?! Who says that?

Everyone I knew—including me—had a mile-long list of things they wanted: more money, more excitement, more love, more stuff, more vacations, more—well, just more.

Hearing someone say that they were happy with their life was a novelty for me.

I was the complete opposite: I felt like I hadn't lived yet. Dying tomorrow would be a catastrophe! I was convinced nothing in my life thus far had been worthwhile. I was wrong, of course, but if all you focus on is everything that's wrong with your life, and how unfair everything is, you will overlook all the good stuff that's there.

Entering in our relationship has simultaneously been the hardest and the easiest thing I have ever done. Easy, because loving Richard and being loved by him feels as natural and simple as breathing.

Hard, because of the obvious: I was so young, and he wasn't. For someone who wanted to fit in so desperately, I wasn't doing a very good job of it.

But that's just it. Nothing I thought I *should* do felt right. It didn't fit. Being with him was the first thing in my adult life that made sense to me. How much did it matter that it made no sense to anyone else?

The thing is, nobody else knows what's best for us. Everybody's opinion is shaped by their own life and their personal experiences, and they can only tell us what they know.

In the end, I realized that listening to my heart and soul has never led me astray, unlike listening to other people did.

I have been following my heart ever since.